Cierra Block

PARIS
BLOCK by BLOCK

(OH)

To Adam,
who is always willing
to go on a pastry safari and
has been my lifelong cheerleader.

Cierra Block

PARIS
BLOCK by BLOCK

Paris block by block

CONTENTS

Arrondissements

of Paris

There is a French word that perfectly encapsulates how to explore Paris: *flâneur*. To *flâneur* you simply must wonder, observe and take in the beauty of the city, and for me there is no better way to explore.

The first time I visited Paris I was 24 years old. My partner and I had been living in London for just over a year and he had a work event in Paris, so I decided to tag along. While he was in meetings during the day, I wandered through museums and department stores, and sat in beautifully landscaped gardens. In the evenings, we would walk along the Seine eating crêpes and trying to time it so that we were at the Eiffel Tower when it lit up on the hour. The following year I went back, but this time with my brother. We decided to stop in at every boulangerie that we passed, trying different baked goods. After this visit, my trips to Paris became an annual event, often meeting up with friends or enjoying a weekend away. My daughter's first trip to Paris took place when she was three months old. We went for a girls' weekend with my mom. With a baby in tow we opted for the smaller museums, walking everywhere as she napped in her buggy and taking numerous breaks charming cafés, truly embracing the art of *flâneur*.

Cierra x

@londonblockbyblock.com
www.londonblockbyblock.com

PARIS

BY FOOD

PART ONE

CHEESE + CHOCOLATE + BAKERIES + COFFEE SHOPS + ICE CREAM
+ FOOD MARKETS + PÂTISSERIES + BRUNCH + CAFÉS & BISTROS
+ CLASSIC DESSERTS + HOT CHOCOLATE + RESTAURANTS

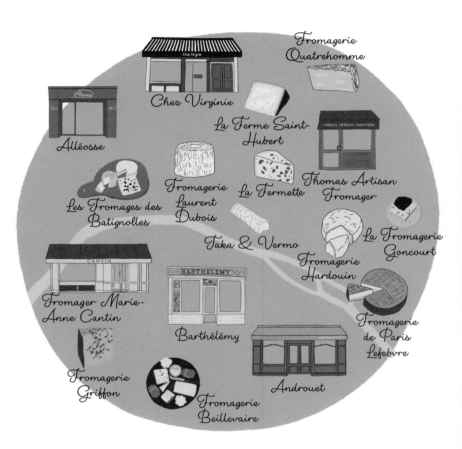

Fromagerie Quatrehomme

Chez Virginie

Alléosse

La Ferme Saint-Hubert

Thomas Artisan Fromager

Fromagerie Laurent Dubois

La Fermette

Les Fromages des Batignolles

Taka & Vermo

La Fromagerie Goncourt

Fromagerie Hardouin

Fromager Marie-Anne Cantin

Barthélémy

Fromagerie de Paris Lefebvre

Fromagerie Griffon

Androuet

Fromagerie Beillevaire

CHEESE

The history of cheese in *France* goes back thousands of years. The first cheeses were made by the Celts and Romans and, over time, French cheesemakers developed their own unique *styles* and flavours, influenced by the climates and terroirs of France. During the Middle Ages, monks became skilled *cheesemakers*, experimenting with different milk types, cultures and ageing methods, and many of the *famous* French cheeses, such as Roquefort and Saint-Nectaire, were invented by monks. France is home to over 1,000 different types of cheese, each with its own unique *flavour and texture*. Whether you are looking for a classic, like brie, or something a bit different, like a Selles-sur-Cher or *Trou du Cru*, you'll be sure to find something delicious at these *fromageries*.

Alléosse
13 Rue Poncelot, 75017, 17th Arr.
A wonderful shop with a wide variety of cheeses from all over France; the staff are happy to help you choose the perfect option for your taste.

Androuet
Multiple locations
As well as selling a large selection of artisanal cheeses, Androuet also offers cheese tastings and cheese-making classes.

Barthélémy
51 Rue de Grenelle, 75007, 7th Arr.
Founded in 1921, this fromagerie holds a certain vintage charm alongside an amazing assortment of French cheeses.

Chez Virginie
Multiple locations
Knowledgeable and passionate cheesemongers since 1946, they specialize in raw-milk cheeses from artisanal producers all over France.

La Ferme Saint-Hubert
36 Rue Marguerite de Rochechouart, 75009, 9th Arr.
Offering cheeses from all over France, as well as further afield. They also have a variety of charcuterie and cheese-adjacent products.

La Fermette
86 Rue Montorgueil, 75002, 2nd Arr.
If you need delicious cheeses, butter, cured meats and jams, this is the place to go. They also sell pre-packaged selection platters.

Fromager Marie-Anne Cantin
12 Rue du Champ de Mars, 75007, 7th Arr.
A higher-end cheese boutique – and you must try their butter.

Fromagerie Beillevaire
Multiple locations
Here, they produce their own high-quality cheeses and butter; you can taste the passion in the cheeses on offer.

La Fromagerie Goncourt
1 Rue Abel Rabaud, 75011, 11th Arr.
An excellent variety of cheeses is available here, with passionate staff.

Fromagerie Griffon
23 bis Avenue de la Motte-Picquet, 75007, 7th Arr.
The cheeses are carefully selected and aged to perfection. Located close to Champ de Mars, it is a great place to pick up delicious cheeses for a picnic.

Fromagerie Hardouin
6 Place d'Aligre, 75012, 12th Arr.
Located in the Marché d'Aligre, with a beautifully curated selection on offer.

Fromagerie Laurent Dubois
Multiple locations
Here, the friendly staff will happily help you find the perfect cheese.

Fromagerie de Paris Lefebvre
229 Rue de Charenton, 75012, 12th Arr.
A small shop that stocks a beautifully curated selection of cheeses.

Fromagerie Quatrehomme
Multiple locations
One of the most awarded cheese shops in Paris, with outstanding choices.

Les Fromages des Batignolles
33 Rue des Moines, 75017, 17th Arr.
Located in the Batignolles covered market, this outlet offers a great selection of French and Italian cheeses.

Taka & Vermo
61 bis Rue du Faubourg Saint-Denis, 75010, 10th Arr.
This small and cosy fromagerie is brimming with great cheeses, including traditional varieties and their own unique homemade creations.

Thomas Artisan Fromager
Multiple locations
Sources the finest cheeses, including classic and more unusual varieties.

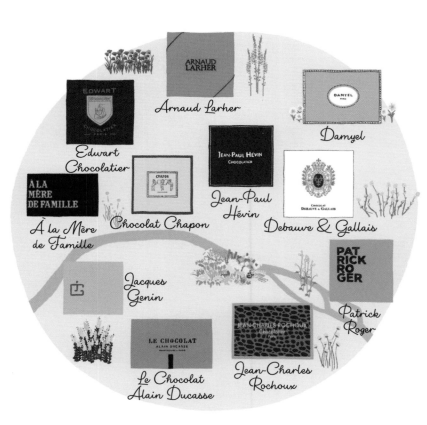

Arnaud Larher

Damyel

Edwart
Chocolatier

Jean-Paul
Hévin

À la Mère
de Famille

Chocolat Chapon

Debauve & Gallais

Patrick
Roger

Jacques
Genin

Le Chocolat
Alain Ducasse

Jean-Charles
Rochoux

CHOCOLATE

Chocolate was first introduced to France in the sixteenth century by the *Spanish*. It was quickly adopted by the French court and nobility, who saw it as a *luxurious* and exotic treat. *Chocolate* was often served as a drink, mixed with spices and other ingredients. The *invention* of the *cocoa press* and advances in mechanization in the late 1800s meant chocolate could be mass-produced and, more importantly, enjoyed by a *wider audience*.

Today, France is one of the leading producers and consumers of chocolate in the world. French chocolate is known for its *high quality* and *innovative* flavours, and is an integral part of French culture.

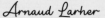

Arnaud Larher

53 Rue Caulaincourt, 75018, 18th Arr.
Sells a wonderful assortment of
handcrafted chocolates, desserts and
macarons. Grab an éclair or dessert to
eat right away, and some chocolate
to enjoy later.

Le Chocolat Alain Ducasse

Multiple locations
Handcrafted bean-to-bar chocolate made in the heart of Paris. This
luxurious French chocolate is packed with flavour.

Chocolat Chapon

69 Rue du Bac, 75007, 7th Arr.
Featuring chocolates from around the world with unique flavours, you
are bound to find something new and delicious here. Don't miss their
chocolate mousse.

Damyel

Multiple locations
A wonderful assortment of chocolate and macarons, all wrapped up in the
loveliest packaging.

Debauve & Gallais

30 Rue des Saints-Pères, 75007, 7th Arr.
Innovators in the chocolate world for over 200 years. It was here that the
first chocolate bar was created, when headache medicine was mixed into
cocoa butter for Queen Marie-Antoinette.

Edwart Chocolatier

Multiple locations
This artisanal chocolate shop also offers chocolate-making workshops,
where you can learn the secrets of making delicious chocolates.

Jacques Genin
Multiple locations

Chocolates and caramels that are simply delicious. Be sure to try the mango passionfruit caramel and the *pâtes de fruit* as well.

Jean-Charles Rochoux
16 Rue d'Assas, 75006, 6th Arr.

Come for the beautiful chocolate sculptures, stay for the unique flavours and melt-in-the-mouth chocolates.

Jean-Paul Hévin
Multiple locations

Beautifully crafted chocolates, macarons and pâtisserie. Best to try a few of everything so you don't miss out on something delicious.

À la Mère de Famille
Multiple locations

Founded in 1761, this is the oldest chocolate shop in Paris. Their selection of chocolates and sweets leaves you spoilt for choice. On a hot day be sure to try their ice cream.

Patrick Roger
Multiple locations

Artisanal chocolate made with unique flavours, plus delightful chocolate sculptures and creatures.

Babka Zana

Mamiche

Du Pain
et des Idées

Poilâne

Le Petit Grain

Clove
Bakery

Aux Merveilleux
de Fred

Momzi
Donuts

Aki
Boulangerie

Blé Sucré

Petite Île
Boulangerie

Sasha
Finklelsztajn

Maison Bergeron

Boulangerie
Bo

Bo & Mie

BAKERIES

Nothing quite beats slicing a fresh loaf of bread – the crack of the crust, the *heavenly* smell of warm dough and the perfect springy texture. When it comes to Paris you are *spoilt for choice* as the city has no shortage of bakeries producing delicious bread and treats, from baguettes to sourdough and *croissants* to kouign-amann. You can find artisan bakeries in every corner of the city, so whether you are looking for a fresh loaf for your picnic, a *pain au chocolat* for breakfast or a brioche to start your weekend, Paris has the perfect *boulangerie* for you, if you know where to look.

Aki Boulangerie
16 Rue Sainte-Anne, 75001, 1st Arr.
A delightful Japanese bakery in the heart of Paris. Try the melon bread or the black sesame éclair.

Aux Merveilleux de Fred
Multiple locations
Go for the chocolate brioche, stay for the delicious meringues.

Babka Zana
Multiple locations
Serving up babkas in a variety of flavours, from halva to pistachio, as well as croissants and pains au chocolat.

Blé Sucré
7 Rue Antoine Vollon, 75012, 12th Arr.
This traditional French bakery serves up all the classics. You really can't go wrong, from the flaky croissants to the fluffy madeleines.

Bo & Mie
Multiple locations
Launched by two bakers, who have won accolades for their creative spins on the classics, they serve incredible cinnamon babkas and eclairs.

Boulangerie Bo
85 bis Rue de Charenton, 75012, 12th Arr.
Nestled in a beautiful art deco building, this bakery has a wonderful selection of traditional baked delights.

Clove Bakery
71 Rue Greneta, 75002, 2nd Arr.
An American-style bakery serving up delicious cookies, cupcakes, brownies and more.

Maison Bergeron
112 Rue Saint-Dominique, 75007, 7th Arr.
A charming bakery with a great aesthetic, offering up a variety of delicious bread and treats.

Mamiche
Multiple locations
Artisanal bread, sandwiches and sweet treats, all baked perfectly.

Momzi Donuts
1 Rue Cherubini, 75002, 2nd Arr.
Doughnut concept bakery with a Parisian twist. Serving innovative flavours, it is a great place to try something new.

Du Pain et des Idées
34 Rue Yves Toudic, 75010, 10th Arr.
This traditional boulangerie bakes all the classics to perfection. From the pistachio snail to the croissant, it is worth the queue.

Le Petit Grain
7 Rue Denoyez, 75020, 20th Arr.
Delicious bread, unique flavours of kouign-amann and cinnamon rolls. What's not to love?

Petite Île Boulangerie
8 Rue des Filles du Calvaire, 75003, 3rd Arr.
A delightful mixture of French and Taiwanese pastries intertwining unique flavours with firm classics.

Poilâne
Multiple locations
Bakers of traditional loaves and sweet treats. It is well worth getting their apple tart.

Sacha Finkelsztajn
27 Rue des Rosiers, 75004, 4th Arr.
Traditional Jewish bakery with a signature yellow-painted shopfront selling babkas, bagels and challah, as well as pastrami sandwiches and more.

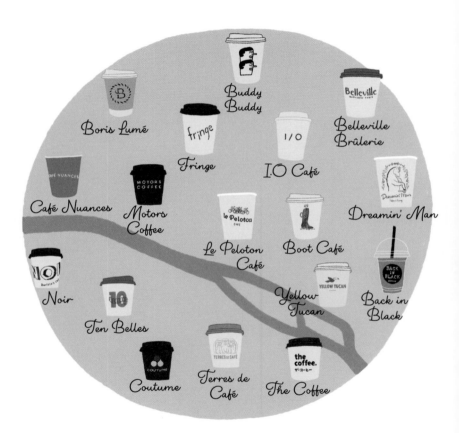

Boris Lumé

Buddy
Buddy

Belleville
Brûlerie

Fringe

I.O Café

Café Nuances

Motors
Coffee

Le Peloton
Café

Boot Café

Dreamin' Man

Noir

Ten Belles

Yellow
Tucan

Back in
Black

Coutume

Terres de
Café

The Coffee

COFFEE SHOPS

The first coffee shop opened in Paris in 1671 (and is still in
business, although it is now *Le Procope* restaurant)
and quickly became a popular meeting place for artists,
writers and *intellectuals*. This started a coffee culture
that expanded in the eighteenth century. People would
gather in coffee houses to discuss *ideas* and debate politics.
During the French Revolution, they were frequented
by political activists and played a key role in spreading
revolutionary ideas. In the late nineteenth and early
twentieth centuries, coffee shops were a symbol of Paris's
intellectual and *cultural life*. Again, artists and *writers*
used these places to meet and share ideas. Today you can still
do this ... or just *enjoy* a cup of coffee!

Back in Black

25 Rue Amelot, 75011, 11th Arr.

Excellent range of handcrafted coffee and great brunch options as well.

Belleville Brûlerie

14 bis Rue Lally-Tollendal, 75019, 19th Arr.

Offering coffee to suit every taste with great attention to detail in the brewing process. Each cup is carefully crafted to bring out the full potential of the beans.

Boot Café

19 Rue du Pont aux Choux, 75003, 3rd Arr.

Cute and cosy café serving up carefully prepared coffee and cookies.

Boris Lumé

28 Rue Lepic, 75018, 18th Arr.

Coffee shop and pâtisserie that is the perfect place to stop for an afternoon pick–me–up.

Buddy Buddy

15 Rue de Marseille, 75010, 10th Arr.

A delicious twist on craft coffee, where every menu item is crafted using nut butters made in-house.

Café Nuances

Multiple locations

Passionate about the perfect coffee with distinctive coffees from around the world.

The Coffee

Multiple locations

Exceptional coffee and a great range of delicious brunch options that are sure to satisfy.

Coutume

47 Rue de Babylone, 75007, 7th Arr.

Inspired by Japan, they have a unique and experimental menu, with drinks you won't find anywhere else.

Dreamin' Man
140 Rue Amelot, 75011, 11th Arr.
Micro espresso bar with a small selection of baked goods that always delight.

Fringe
106 Rue de Turenne, 75003, 3rd Arr.
Great coffee, tasty house-made granola and delicious banana bread.

I.O Café
16 Rue Dupetit-Thouars, 75003, 3rd Arr.
Pastries and coffee are served up in this quaint shop.

Motors Coffee
7 Rue des Halles, 75001, 1st Arr.
Great coffee using unique and flavoursome European roasted coffee beans.

Noir
Multiple locations
Speciality coffee and yummy pastries and cookies.

Le Peloton Café
17 Rue du Pont Louis-Philippe, 75004, 4th Arr.
Delicious coffee, waffles and filled croissants.

Ten Belles
Multiple locations
A variety of pastries, quick bites and speciality coffees.

Terres de Café
Multiple locations
They roast their coffee in-house and bake delicious banana bread
and cookies.

Yellow Tucan
20 Rue des Tournelles, 75004, 4th Arr.
Delightful coffee shop serving artisan coffees, fresh-pressed juices
and baked goods.

Bachir

Glaces
Glazed

À la Mère
de Famille

Une Glace
à Paris

Bältis

Grom

La Glace
Alain Ducasse

Martine Lambert
Glaces et Sorbets

Berthillon

+82 Paris

Le Bac
à Glaces

Gelati
d'Alberto

ICE CREAM

Ice cream has been enjoyed in Paris for centuries.
The first ice cream-like desserts were introduced to France
by *Catherine de' Medici,* who brought the recipe with
her from Italy when she married Henry II of *France*
in 1533. Those early desserts were made with snow and
ice, which were *flavoured* with fruits, *spices and honey.*
Ice cream has since evolved as tastes and production
techniques have changed and as people from around the
world brought new flavours with them. You can find a
wonderful selection of these *cooling treats* across the
city, from traditional sorbets to gelatos to
ice creams and shaved ice.

Le Bac à Glaces
109 Rue du Bac, 75007, 7th Arr.
Delightful little ice cream café serving old-school sundaes as well as new concoctions.

Bachir
Multiple locations
This Lebanese-inspired ice cream shop is known for topping its wares with generous quantities of pistachio and whipped cream.

Bältis
Multiple locations
Ice cream in unique flavours such as halva, ashta and rosewater, as well as refreshing sorbets.

Berthillon
31 and 46 Rue Saint-Louis en l'Île, 75004, 4th Arr.
Known for its traditional French ice cream with a rich and creamy texture; there are over 80 flavours of ice cream and sorbet available here.

La Glace Alain Ducasse
38 Rue de la Roquette, 75011, 11th Arr.
Extraordinary ice cream dreamed up by expert chocolatier Alain Ducasse.

Une Glace à Paris
Multiple locations
Great ice creams and sorbets with unusual, but delicious, flavours to sample.

Glaces Glazed
Multiple locations

This artisanal ice cream shop has exciting flavour combinations that are perfectly balanced.

Gelati d'Alberto
45 Rue Mouffetard, 75005, 5th Arr.

This ice cream parlour has a wide variety of classic and original flavours, all served beautifully scooped into a flower.

Grom
Multiple locations

Paris outposts of this beloved Italian chain, offering up wonderful flavours of gelato.

Martine Lambert Glaces et Sorbets
39 Rue Cler, 75007, 7th Arr.

Delicious ice cream made in-house using natural ingredients.

À la Mère de Famille
Multiple locations

The oldest chocolate shop in Paris also serves up delicious ice cream.

+82 Paris
11 bis Rue Vauquelin, 75005, 5th Arr.

This Korean café has a delicious bingsu, a milky shaved ice dessert topped with fruit. Try the mango.

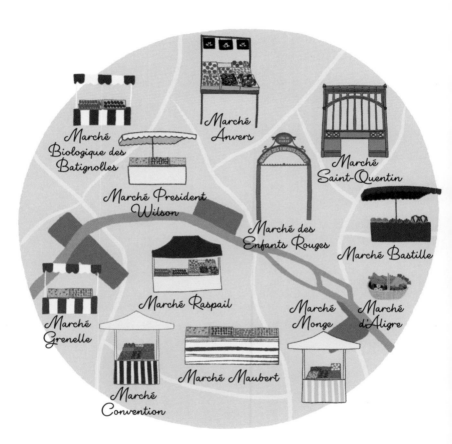

Marché Anvers

Marché Biologique des Batignolles

Marché Saint-Quentin

Marché Président Wilson

Marché des Enfants Rouges

Marché Bastille

Marché Raspail

Marché Grenelle

Marché Monge

Marché d'Aligre

Marché Maubert

Marché Convention

FOOD MARKETS

PARIS BY FOOD

Farmers markets have been a staple of French culture since the fifteenth century. They are *social events* that provide a sense of community as well as a popular way for *Parisians* to buy fresh local produce and speciality food such as cheeses, *charcuterie, bread* and *meat*. There are over 100 farmers' markets held in Paris every week. Each market has its own operating hours, so check before you go. *Wandering* around these markets gives you a wonderful sense of the *devotion* to quality of French food producers.

Marché Anvers

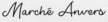

Place d'Anvers, 75009, 9th Arr.
Small Friday market with local delights and high-quality products.

Marché d'Aligre

Rue d'Aligre, 75012, 12th Arr.
This large market is open Tuesday through Sunday. The covered section hosts butchers, cheeses and wine, as well as prepared food.

Marché Bastille

2018 Blvd Richard-Lenoir, 75011, 11th Arr.
Open Thursdays and Sundays, this market has a wonderful selection of produce, cheese, wine and more.

Marché Biologique des Batignolles

34 Blvd des Batignolles, 75017, 17th Arr.
This Saturday market carries only organic products and is a true gastronomic experience.

Marché Convention

Rue de la Convention, 75015, 15th Arr.
Open Tuesday, Thursday and Sunday, this local market has a wonderful selection of fresh produce, cheeses, bread, charcuterie and more.

Marché des Enfants Rouges

39 Rue de Bretagne, 75003, 3rd Arr.
Founded in 1615, this market is open every day except Monday. Boasting an eclectic selection of street food, it's a great place to grab lunch.

Marché Grenelle
Blvd de Grenelle, 75015, 15th Arr.

Open Wednesday and Sunday, this market has a great selection of fresh fruits and vegetables, as well as some snacks you can eat on the go.

Marché Maubert
35 Place Maubert, 75005, 5th Arr.

Open Tuesday, Thursday and Saturday, this great little market has excellent quality produce fresh from the farm and a must-visit bakery.

Marché Monge
1 Place Monge, 75005, 5th Arr.

A great market in central Paris with incredibly fresh produce, seafood, flowers, and more. Open Wednesday, Friday and Sunday.

Marché Raspail
Blvd Raspail, 75006, 6th Arr.

Open Tuesday and Sunday, this typical French street market has a great selection of fruit and vegetable stalls, cheese, meat and freshly prepared ready-to-eat food.

Marché Saint-Quentin
85 bis Blvd de Magenta, 75010, 10th Arr.

Open every day except Monday, this covered market has a great selection of quick bites, flowers, sushi and more.

Marché Président Wilson
Avenue du Président Wilson, 75116, 16th Arr.

Open Wednesday and Saturday, this fantastic farmers' market offers fresh produce from local producers with a top-tier selection of vegetables, meats, fish, cheese, flowers, bread and more.

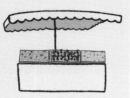

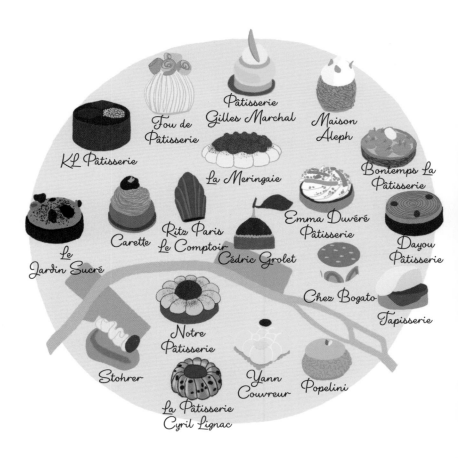

Fou de
Pâtisserie

Pâtisserie
Gilles Marchal

Maison
Aleph

KL Pâtisserie

La Meringaie

Bontemps La
Pâtisserie

Le
Jardin Sucré

Carette

Ritz Paris
Le Comptoir

Emma Duvéré
Pâtisserie

Dayou
Pâtisserie

Cédric Grolet

Chez Bogato

Tapisserie

Stohrer

Notre
Pâtisserie

Yann
Couvreur

Popelini

La Pâtisserie
Cyril Lignac

PÂTISSERIES

The first pâtisserie was opened in 1730 by Nicolas Stohrer, pastry chef to *King Louis XV*. Still in operation today, Stohrer's pâtisserie introduced a world of new *desserts and possibilities*. In the centuries since, French chefs have developed unique styles of pastry-making, characterized by the use of *high-quality ingredients*, fine attention to detail and a strong emphasis on creativity. These chefs are always looking for new and innovative ways to create and are not afraid to experiment with *different flavours*, ingredients or methods, which is why they are so often *unique and interesting*. French pâtisserie is enjoyed all over the world, but there is nothing quite like experiencing it first-hand in Paris.

Bontemps La Pâtisserie
Multiple locations
Known for its delicate pastries and signature sables.

Carette
Multiple locations
This famous tearoom is renowned for its traditional French pâtisserie served in an elegant atmosphere.

Chez Bogato
5 Rue Saint-Merri, 75004, 4th Arr.
A playful pâtisserie serving up creative and festive cakes.

Dayou Pâtisserie
42 R. Bréguet, 75011, 11th Arr.
Elegant and delicious pastries that look almost too good to eat.

Emma Duvéré Pâtisserie
41 Rue Sedaine, 75011, 11th Arr.
Traditional and modern treats are on offer here.

Fou de Pâtisserie
Multiple locations
Wonderful place to enjoy delicious gâteaux.

Le Jardin Sucré
156 Rue de Courcelles, 75017, 17th Arr.
A delightful pâtisserie offering a selection of macarons, pastries and other sweet treats.

KL Pâtisserie
78 Avenue de Villiers, 75017, 17th Arr.
Offering a delicious and modern take on classic French pâtisserie.

Maison Aleph
Multiple locations
A fusion of French techniques with Middle Eastern flavours.

La Meringaie
Multiple locations
Known for its light, airy meringues made fresh with seasonal ingredients.

Notre Pâtisserie
7 Rue Amélie, 75007, 7th Arr.
Outstanding traditional pâtisserie, as well as its more innovative creations.

La Pâtisserie Cyril Lignac
Multiple locations
This award-winning pâtisserie does not disappoint.

Pâtisserie Gilles Marchal
9 Rue Ravignan, 75018, 18th Arr.
Decisions, decisions ... when everything looks this good, you can't get it wrong.

La Pâtisserie du Meurice par Cédric Grolet
6 Rue de Castiglione, 75001, 1st Arr.
The world-renowned pastry chef is known for his innovative desserts.

Popelini
Multiple locations
Little choux pastries that are filled with the most incredible flavours.

Ritz Paris Le Comptoir
38 Rue Cambon, 75001, 1st Arr.
An assortment of delights is available here, from madeleines to gâteaux.

Stohrer
Multiple locations
Come for the history, stay for the delicious desserts.

Tapisserie
65 Rue de Charonne, 75011, 11th Arr.
A petite pâtisserie whisking up incredible flans, tarts, choux and more.

Yann Couvreur
Multiple locations
The Paris-Brest is a bestseller for a reason, but everything is good here.

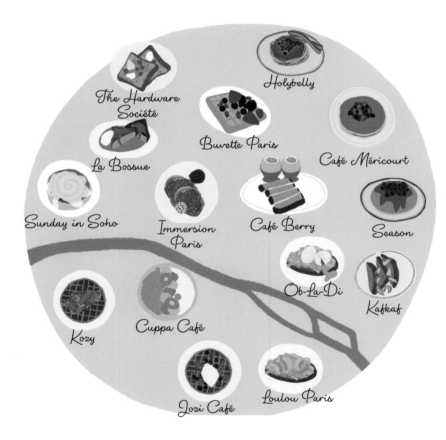

The Hardware Société

Holybelly

Buvette Paris

Café Méricourt

La Bossue

Sunday in Soho

Immersion Paris

Café Berry

Season

Ob-La-Di

Kafkaf

Kozy

Cuppa Café

Jozi Café

Loulou Paris

BRUNCH

Brunching culture in Paris is a relatively new *phenomenon* but it has become an increasingly popular meal, especially at weekends. There is something *quintessentially* French about taking time to enjoy a leisurely meal and brunch is the *perfect opportunity* to do that. With an influx of flavours and dishes from around the world, you can find places to brunch that have *American favourites* such as pancakes and waffles, Aussie delights such as *avo toast* and banana bread and wonderful new *creations* inspired by French cuisine.

Café Berry

10 Rue Chapon, 75003, 3rd Arr.
A *petite* café with delicious brunch options,
including French toast, pancakes and
house-made granola.

La Bossue

9 Rue Joseph de Maistre, 75018, 18th Arr.
Enjoy weekend brunch at this charming neighbourhood bakery.

Buvette Paris

28 Rue Henry Monnier, 75009, 9th Arr.
Serving up classic French dishes and waffles.

Café Méricourt

22 Rue de la Folie Méricourt, 75011, 11th Arr.
Great brunch spot with shakshuka, pancakes, granola and more on offer.

Cuppa Café

86 Rue de l'Université, 75007, 7th Arr.
Quaint spot for brunch serving classic brunch dishes with a slight Asian twist.

The Hardware Société

10 Rue Lamarck, 75018, 18th Arr.
Serving up Aussie-style brunch in a charming location.

Holybelly

5 Rue Lucien Sampaix, 75010, 10th Arr.
From eggs to pancakes and granola to avocado toast, a great selection.

Immersion Paris

Multiple locations

From sweet to savoury, there is something for everyone here.

Jozi Café

3 Rue Valette, 75005, 5th Arr.

Amazing pancakes and delicious viennoiserie.

Kafkaf

7 Rue Keller, 75011, 11th Arr.

Great eggs benedict as well as fluffy pistachio pancakes.

Kozy

Multiple locations

From savoury pancakes to chicken and waffles, there are lots of delicious menu items here.

Loulou Paris

90 Blvd Saint-Germain, 75005, 5th Arr.

Aussie-style brunch served in the heart of the Latin Quarter.

Ob-La-Di

54 Rue de Saintonge, 75003, 3rd Arr.

Serving up banana bread, granola bowls, avo toast and delicious scones.

Season

67 Rue St Sabin, 75011, 11th Arr.

Try the eggs benedict, fluffy pancakes or an acai bowl.

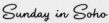

Sunday in Soho

7 Rue Saint-Marc, 75002, 2nd Arr.

Be sure to try their cinnamon rolls, available at the weekend.

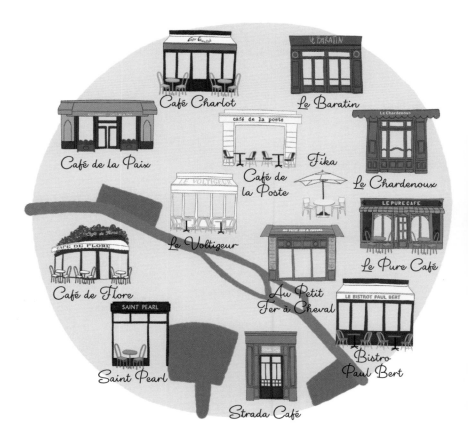

Café Charlot

Le Baratin

Café de la Paix

café de la poste

Café de la Poste

Tika

Le Chardenoux

Le Voltigeur

Au Petit Fer à Cheval

Le Pure Café

Café de Flore

SAINT PEARL

LE BISTROT PAUL BERT

Bistro Paul Bert

Saint Pearl

Strada Café

CAFÉS & BISTROS

PARIS BY FOOD

Café culture has been a way of life in Paris since the first café opened in the 1600s. *Parisian* cafés are typically quite *small and intimate* and can be found on almost every corner (there are over 1,500 in the city). Local bistros, often *family-run*, are the perfect places to enjoy the ambience of the city while enjoying a *glass of wine* alongside classic French dishes.

Le Baratin
3 Rue Jouye-Rouve, 75020, 20th Arr.
This modern bistro serves classic dishes, executed to perfection.

Bistrot Paul Bert
18 Rue Paul Bert, 75011, 11th Arr.
Quintessential Parisian bistro serving up classics such as steaks, soufflés and scallops.

Café Charlot
38 Rue de Bretagne, 75003, 3rd Arr.
From breakfast to late-night dinner, you can enjoy a delightful French meal here.

Café de Flore
172 Blvd Saint-Germain, 75006, 6th Arr.
This café is extremely popular with tourists, with good reason. The food is decent and the hot chocolate is great.

Café de la Paix
5 Place de l'Opéra, 75009, 9th Arr.
With views of the Opera House, it is hard not to be enchanted by this café serving traditional French fare and decadent desserts.

Café de la Poste
124 Rue de Turenne, 75003, 3rd Arr.
Serving up international dishes and French classics, it is a great spot for a meal any time of the day.

Fika

11 Rue Payenne, 75003, 3rd Arr.
Located in the courtyard of the Swedish
Institute, this Swedish café is a great
option for lunch or a coffee.

Le Chardenoux

1 Rue Jules Vallès, 75011, 11th Arr.
In operation since 1908, this charming bistro has amazing lobster rolls
and mouth-watering desserts.

Au Petit Fer à Cheval

30 Rue Vieille-du-Temple, 75004, 4th Arr.
Chic but unpretentious bistro with a well-curated menu of French
favourites, all served in a cosy ambience.

Le Pure Café

14 Rue Jean-Macé, 75011, 11th Arr.
This old-fashioned bistro has charming décor and a great selection of food.

Saint Pearl

38 Rue des Saints-Pères, 75007, 7th Arr.
Come for the charming atmosphere, stay for the matcha roll!

Strada Café

Multiple locations
A great café to enjoy brunch or a quick coffee.

Le Voltigeur

45 Rue des Francs Bourgeois, 75004, 4th Arr.
A charming café with amazing hot chocolate and freshly pressed juices.

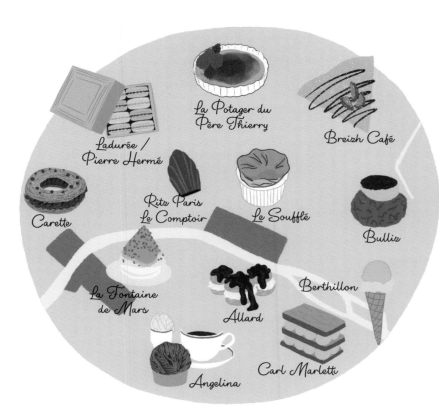

Ladurée / Pierre Hermé

La Potager du Père Thierry

Breizh Café

Carette

Ritz Paris Le Comptoir

Le Soufflé

Bulliz

La Fontaine de Mars

Allard

Berthillon

Angelina

Carl Marletti

CLASSIC DESSERTS

PARIS BY FOOD

France is famous the world over for its *decadent desserts* made with high-quality ingredients and exceptional attention to detail. From smooth custards to whipped *Chantilly cream,* and from flaky pastry to perfectly ripe fruit tarts, the French have truly *perfected the art* of making desserts. Here are some of the best desserts the *French* introduced to the world, with suggestions of where to try them. Don't let this map limit you though: let it be an *inspiration to taste,* explore and ultimately discover your own favourites.

Hot Chocolate and Mont Blanc

Angelina, multiple locations
Serving up a rich thick hot chocolate with ample whipped cream, Angelina is a must-try for chocolate lovers. Pair with their perfectly proportioned Mont Blanc (a dessert made with chestnut purée 'vermicelli' and cream) for a delicious duo.

Choux Bun

Bulliz, 14 Rue d'Hauteville, 75010, 10th Arr.
These delightful bite-sized pastries are fluffy and light and packed with the most delicious cream and flavoured fillings.

Crème Brûlée

Le Potager du Père Thierry, 16 Rue des Trois Frères, 75018, 18th Arr.
This quaint restaurant in Montmartre serves up classic French dishes, and their crème brûlée is not to be missed.

Crêpes

Breizh Café, multiple locations
Instead of deciding between a savoury galette or a sweet crêpe, it is best just to order one of each!

Ice Cream

Berthillon, 31 and 46 Rue Saint Louis en l'Île, 75004, 4th Arr.
Beloved by locals and tourists alike. The ice cream here is worth the queue.

Île Flottante

La Fontaine de Mars, 129 Rue Saint-Dominique, 75007, 7th Arr.
The île flottante is especially worth trying at this classic French restaurant, where traditional desserts are made to perfection.

Madeleines

Ritz Paris Le Comptoir, 38 Rue Cambon, 75001, 1st Arr.
Pick from a variety of perfectly flavoured madeleines in the delightful ambience of the Ritz's bakery.

Millefeuille

Carl Marletti, 51 Rue Censier, 75005, 5th Arr.
Perfectly layered, the millefeuille here is well worth trying (but everything here is delicious, so it's wise to get an assortment).

Paris-Brest

Carette, 25 Place des Vosges, 75003, 3rd Arr.
Hazelnut cream and flaky pastry are combined to create an absolutely delectable dessert.

Profiteroles

Allard, 41 Rue Saint-André des Arts, 75006, 6th Arr.
Step back in time at this charming bistro serving up classic French dishes, and stay for the profiteroles.

Soufflé

Le Soufflé, 36 Rue du Mont Thabor, 75001, 1st Arr.
Enjoy an entire meal where everything is souffléd. From savoury mains to sweet desserts, this is a place to not be missed.

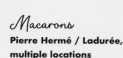

Macarons

**Pierre Hermé / Ladurée,
multiple locations**
When it comes to macarons, your first visit should be to Pierre Hermé or Ladurée. Why not try macarons from both and decide which is your favourite?

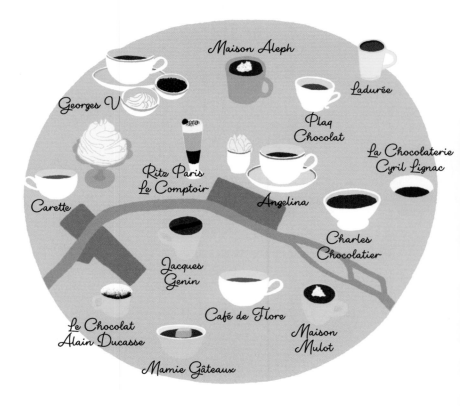

Maison Aleph

Georges V

Ladurée

Plaq
Chocolat

La Chocolaterie
Cyril Lignac

Ritz Paris
Le Comptoir

Angelina

Carette

Charles
Chocolatier

Jacques
Genin

Café de Flore

Le Chocolat
Alain Ducasse

Maison
Mulot

Mamie Gâteaux

HOT CHOCOLATE

Hot chocolate, or *chocolat chaud* in French, is *something special* and not quite like hot chocolate you will find anywhere else. In Paris, it is made with high-quality chocolate that is rich and flavourful, giving the drink its decadent and *distinct taste*. The chocolate to milk ratio is also higher than elsewhere, making for a thicker and *more luxurious* hot chocolate that simply must be savoured slowly. It is often topped off with *whipped cream* and enjoyed in a cosy café, with some pâtisserie completing the *experience*.

Angelina

Multiple locations

Decedent hot chocolate at its finest,
served with all the accompaniments
one could wish for.

Café de Flore

172 Blvd Saint-Germain, 75006, 6th Arr.

Thick and luxurious hot chocolate served in an iconic café that is perfect
for people-watching.

Carette

25 Place des Vosges, 75003, 3rd Arr.

A rich, creamy, chocolatey delight that is sure to satisfy your sweet tooth.

Charles Chocolatier

15 Rue Montorgueil, 75001, 1st Arr.

Serving up luxurious hot chocolates that are perfectly delicious.

Le Chocolat Alain Ducasse

Multiple locations

Indulgent hot chocolate, best served with a side of chocolate cake.
There's a hot-chocolate mix to make at home too.

La Chocolaterie Cyril Lignac

25 Rue Chanzy, 75011, 11th Arr.

Serving up chocolate with more chocolate. Pair a hot chocolate with
another chocolatey dessert.

Georges V
31 Avenue George V, 75008, 8th Arr.
A culinary masterpiece that is sure to impress, despite its cost at this high-end hotel.

Jacques Genin
Multiple locations
The decadent hot chocolate here is a chocolate lover's dream.

Ladurée
Multiple locations
Here you can find a rich and flavourful drink that is perfect for pairing with a few of their signature macarons.

Maison Aleph
Multiple locations
A hot chocolate not to be missed; add any of the delicious pastries on offer for the perfect combo.

Maison Mulot
76 Rue de Seine, 2 Rue Lobineau, 75006, 6th Arr.
The indulgent hot chocolate here is sure to please even the most discerning chocolate lover.

Mamie Gâteaux
66 Rue du Cherche-Midi, 75006, 6th Arr.
Warm and rich, the hot chocolate here tastes like a comforting hug.

Plaq Chocolat
4 Rue du Nil, 75002, 2nd Arr.
The hot chocolate here is a real treat for the senses.

Ritz Paris Le Comptoir
38 Rue Cambon, 75001, 1st Arr.
A must-try hot chocolate made the old fashioned way – a really extravagant experience and special treat.

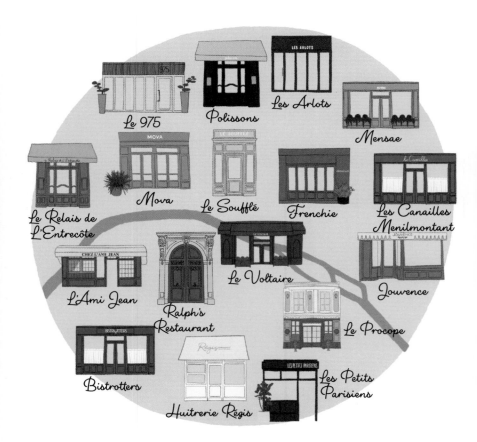

Le 975

Polissons

Les Arlots

Mensae

Le Relais de
L'Entrecôte

Mova

Le Soufflé

Frenchie

Les Canailles
Menilmontant

L'Ami Jean

Ralph's
Restaurant

Le Voltaire

Jouvence

Bistrotters

Huitrerie Régis

Les Petits
Parisiens

Le Procope

RESTAURANTS

Paris is packed with amazing restaurants that pride themselves on *leisurely meals* made with quality ingredients that diners can savour without being rushed. Restaurant culture is strong in this city, with eating out seen as the perfect way to *relax and socialize*. You can have an amazing lunch at a small, inexpensive brasserie – or in a *Michelin-starred* restaurant. Whatever your budget, you are sure to enjoy *memorable meals*. Take your time, savour the atmosphere, and remember it is *always a good idea* to order dessert.

L'Ami Jean
27 Rue Malar, 75007, 7th Arr.
A classic Parisian bistro serving dishes in a cosy, old-fashioned setting.

Les Arlots
136 Rue du Faubourg Poissonnière, 75010, 10th Arr.
Bistro offering traditional specialities in a warm, intimate atmosphere.

Bistrotters
9 Rue Decrès, 75014, 14th Arr.
A charming bistro serving up French delights cooked to perfection.

Les Canailles Menilmontant
15 Rue des Panoyaux, 75020, 20th Arr.
Offering impeccable service and food in a classic bistro setting.

Frenchie
5 Rue du Nil, 75002, 2nd Arr.
A cosy Michelin-starred restaurant with a seasonal tasting menu.

Huitrerie Régis
3 Rue de Montfaucon, 75006, 6th Arr.
This snug restaurant offers up the freshest seafood platters and accompaniments.

Jouvence
172 bis Rue du Faubourg Saint-Antoine, 75012, 12th Arr.
A charming neo-bistro with creative food served in an inviting atmosphere.

Mensae
23 Rue Melingue, 75019, 19th Arr.
Whether you pick the à la carte or set menu, don't miss the chocolate mousse.

Mova
39 Rue des Dames, 75017, 17th Arr.
Enjoy a set menu or tasting menu offering consistently amazing dishes in a welcoming atmosphere.

Le 975

185 Rue Marcadet 75018, 18th Arr.

Creative, seasonal cuisine enjoyed in a pared-down, friendly atmosphere.

Les Petits Parisiens

49 Avenue Jean Moulin, 75014, 14th Arr.

A quaint and cosy bistro serving up quintessential French dishes.

Polissons

35 Rue Ramey, 75018, 18th Arr.

A great place to enjoy some bistro-gastronomy.

Le Procope

13 Rue de l'Ancienne Comédie, 75006, 6th Arr.

A timeless institution that has been serving up delicious food and wine for generations.

Ralph's Restaurant

173 Blvd Saint-Germain, 75006, 6th Arr.

Enjoy classic American dishes in this stately restaurant at Ralph Lauren's flagship store.

Le Relais de L'Entrecôte

Multiple locations

They serve only steak and frites, so you will only have to choose what you want for dessert.

Le Soufflé

36 Rue du Mont Thabor, 75001, 1st Arr.

Sweet and savoury soufflés can be enjoyed in this charming restaurant.

Le Voltaire

27 Quai Voltaire, 75007, 7th Arr.

Traditional French cuisine can be enjoyed in Voltaire's former Paris home.

PARIS

BY LOCALS

PART TWO

CANAL SAINT-MARTIN + THE MARAIS + THE LATIN QUARTER

+ ÎLE DE LA CITÉ & ÎLE SAINT-LOUIS + SAINT-GERMAIN-DES-PRÉS +

RUE DU BAC + MONTMARTRE + THE SEINE + OPÉRA + LOUVRE

+ BASTILLE + BOIS DE BOULOGNE

Marrow

Candide

Taka & Vermo

DWICH & GLACE

Dwich & Glace

Café Margot

COLONEL

Colonel

La Tarte au Carré

ARTAZART

Artazart

Bulliz

Du Pain et des Idées

Kubo Pâtisserie

Centre Commercial Kids

Buddy Buddy

LA TRÉSORERIE

La Trésorerie

CANAL SAINT-MARTIN
10TH ARRONDISSEMENT

This *vibrant and diverse* neighbourhood has an abundance of charming cafés and *galleries* dotting the Saint-Martin Canal. A trendy area full of tree-lined streets and *independent* shops, it has a high concentration of coffee shops as well. The atmosphere here is *more relaxed* that other parts of the city and you will find a good mix of locals and tourists, often sitting by the canal enjoying drinks or a *small picnic with friends*. Whether you are looking for a night out on the town, a day of *exploring* museums or a relaxing stroll by the water, the 10th arrondissement has something for everyone.

Artazart
83 Quai de Valmy, 75010, 10th Arr.
Here you will find a treasure trove of design
books, magazines, and gifts for the creative soul.

Buddy Buddy
15 Rue de Marseille, 75010, 10th Arr.
A unique vegan coffee shop where every drink is infused with nut butter.

Bulliz
14 Rue d'Hauteville, 75010, 10th Arr.
Specializing in choux pastries, this is a great place to stop in for coffee
and sweet treats.

Café Margo
12 Avenue Richerand, 75010, 10th Arr.
A quaint café with great coffee and a wonderful selection of food.

Candide
35 Rue de Sambre-et-Meuse, 75010, 10th Arr.
A charming restaurant with inventive sharing plates served in
a modern setting.

Centre Commercial Kids
22 Rue Yves Toudic, 75010, 10th Arr.
A great kids' shop with a wonderful curation of clothes, shoes
and accessories.

Colonel
14 Avenue Richerand, 75010, 10th Arr.
Upscale modern homeware in a light and airy shop.

Dwich & Glace
22 Rue des Vinaigriers, 75010, 10th Arr.
Mouth-watering vegan sandwiches and quick bites, steps away from the canal itself.

Kubo Pâtisserie
25 Rue Jacques Louvel-Tessier, 75010, 10th Arr.
Artisanal pastries, each made with a perfect harmony of flavours, in a small neighbourhood shop.

Marrow
128 Rue du Faubourg Saint-Martin, 75010, 10th Arr.
From preparation to presentation, everything here is cooked and flavoured to perfection.

Du Pain et des Idées
34 Rue Yves Toudic, 75010, 10th Arr.
Boasting a century and a half in business, this bakery has a beautiful interior and equally delicious baked goods.

Taka & Vermo
61 bis Rue du Faubourg Saint-Denis, 75010, 10th Arr.
Artisan fromagerie with a great selection of cheeses and knowledgeable, helpful staff.

La Tarte au Carré
38 Rue du Château d'Eau, 75010, 10th Arr.
Enjoy a small selection of sweet and savoury tarts, quiche, and more – all baked in squares!

La Trésorerie
11 Rue du Château d'Eau, 75010, 10th Arr.
Kitchen and interiors shop with beautiful ceramics and a wonderful assortment of trinkets for the home.

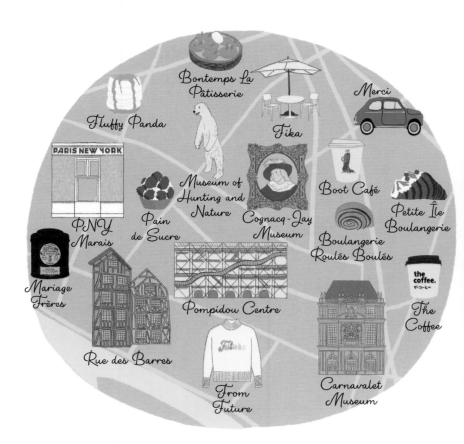

Fluffy Panda

Bontemps La
Pâtisserie

Fika

Merci

PARIS NEW YORK

Museum of
Hunting and
Nature

Boot Café

Petite Île
Boulangerie

PNY
Marais

Pain
de Sucre

Cognacq-Jay
Museum

Boulangerie
Roulés Boulés

Mariage
Frères

Pompidou Centre

The
Coffee

Rue des Barres

From
Future

Carnavalet
Museum

THE MARAIS
3RD & 4TH ARRONDISSEMENTS

PARIS BY LOCALS

This *historic area* is one of the most popular with tourists and loved by residents as well. With its eclectic history and a mix of *old and new* (the oldest houses in Paris are in the Marais), it is no wonder. The area was once home to *aristocrats* and their large properties have long since been repurposed into smaller homes and business premises. With a wealth of bakeries, restaurants, shops, *history and museums*, it has much to offer every visitor. Some streets can get quite crowded with tourists, but there are lots of *lovely corners* and squares offering respite from the hustle and bustle.

Bontemps La Pâtisserie
57 Rue de Bretagne, 75003, 3rd Arr.
Enjoy delightful deserts and tea in the secret garden of this restaurant and pretend you're in the countryside.

Boot Café
19 Rue du Pont aux Choux, 75003, 3rd Arr.
Bite-sized coffee shop serving delightful cookies alongside artisanal roasts.

Boulangerie Roulés Boulés
1 bis Rue Saint-Gilles, 75003, 3rd Arr.
Pick up a treat and enjoy it in the Arnaud Beltrame garden across the road.

Carnavalet Museum
23 Rue de Sévigné, 75003, 3rd Arr.
Housed in two Renaissance mansions, this museum explores the history of Paris.

The Coffee
2 Rue Saint-Gilles, 75003, 3rd Arr.
Minimalist café passionate about making perfect cups of coffee, served alongside sweet bites.

Cognacq-Jay Museum
8 Rue Elzevir, 75003, 3rd Arr.
Known for its elegant setting and impressive, once private collection of fine art, this museum is a joy to explore.

Fika
11 Rue Payenne, 75003, 3rd Arr.
Step into the charming Fika café to enjoy Nordic pastries and sandwiches.

Fluffy Panda
22 Rue Réaumur, 75003, 3rd Arr.
Perfectly fluffy Japanese-style soufflé pancakes with toothsome toppings.

From Future
7 Rue des Rosiers, 75004, 4th Arr.
Cheerful cashmere jumpers and cardigans, sustainably produced.

Mariage Frères
30 Rue du Bourg Tibourg, 75004, 4th Arr.
Creating fine tea blends since 1854, this is a must-visit for any tea lover.

Merci
111 Blvd Beaumarchais, 75003, 3rd Arr.
This charming shop is known for the red Fiat 500 parked outside. Inside, you'll find a thoughtful curation of homeware.

Museum of Hunting and Nature
62 Rue des Archives, 75003, 3rd Arr.
A museum that uses the history of hunting to explore our relationship with nature. Expect taxidermied animals, paintings and much more.

Pain de Sucre
14 Rue Rambuteau, 75003, 3rd Arr.
This pâtisserie offers artistic desserts as well as savoury lunch dishes.

Petite Île Boulangerie
8 Rue des Filles du Calvaire, 75003, 3rd Arr.
Delightful boulangerie with an unusual double chocolate pain au chocolat and filled croissants.

PNY Marais
10 Rue Sainte-Croix de la Bretonnerie, 75004, 4th Arr.
An awesome burger restaurant in the heart of the Marais serving up American-style patties.

Pompidou Centre
Place Georges-Pompidou, 75004, 4th Arr.
Home to the largest collection of modern art in Europe, where the building is as much part of the art as the collection.

Rue des Barres
75004, 4th Arr.
Charming street with medieval houses at one end and cafés and restaurants at the other.

Le Reminet

Le Caveau de
la Huchette

Shakespeare
and Company

The Abbey
Bookshop

Jardin
des Plantes

Panthéon

Arenas of Lutetia

Rue Mouffetard

THE LATIN QUARTER
5TH ARRONDISSEMENT

PARIS BY LOCALS

A *vibrant pocket* of Paris since the Roman times, the
Latin Quarter is so called because at the *Sorbonne*,
the *oldest university* in France, tuition was originally
given in Latin, which was the main academic language
in Europe during the Middle Ages. Millennia before this,
Romans enjoyed entertainment at an *amphitheatre*,
whose ruins can still be seen today. On top of this
history there are lovely parks and *amazing food* options,
making it a *unique* area to explore.

The Abbey Bookshop
29 Rue de la Parcheminerie, 75005, 5th Arr.

A treasure trove of English-language books in the heart of Paris selling new, used and rare tomes.

Arenas of Lutetia
49 Rue Monge, 75005, 5th Arr.

A Roman amphitheatre turned public square in the heart of Paris (known in Roman times as Lutetia). The steps of this arena are a great place to enjoy lunch, or a little afternoon treat.

Le Caveau de la Huchette
5 Rue de la Huchette, 75005, 5th Arr.

Legendary jazz club that has been host to some of the biggest names in jazz. A visit here is sure to be a night to remember.

Jardin des Plantes
75 Rue Cuvier, 75005, 5th Arr.

This garden is a true gem and full of lovely ways to spend a day. Featuring three museums, the Gallery of Mineralogy and Geology, the National Museum of Natural History and the Gallery of Paleontology, it also boasts a zoo, a beautiful botanical garden and a delightful animal-themed carousel.

Panthéon
Place du Panthéon, 75005, 5th Arr.
This neoclassical church and mausoleum houses the remains of some of France's most illustrious figures.

Le Reminet
3 Rue des Grands Degrés, 75005, 5th Arr.
A charming bistro offering a contemporary take on classic French dishes.

Rue Mouffetard
75005, 5th Arr.
This charming street is dotted with pâtisseries, cafés, boulangeries and shops. Some favourite places are Pâtisserie David Doualan, Fromagerie Androuet, Tcham restaurant, Boulangerie Liberté, Les Crêpes de Louis-Marie, Graines du Jour, Café Dose and Gelati d'Alberto.

Shakespeare and Company
37 Rue de la Bûcherie, 75005, 5th Arr.
Located in the heart of the Latin Quarter this bookshop is a must-visit for any book lover in Paris. It is filled with an eclectic selection of reading matter and known for its strong literary history.

Square du
Vert-Galant

Pont Neuf

Restaurant
Paul

Atelier du Geste
à l'Émotion

Sainte-
Chapelle

Notre-Dame
Cathedral

Pâtisserie
Tourbillon
Saint Louis

La Ferme
Saint-Aubin

Berthillon

Deportation
Memorial

Minicafé

Square
Barye

ÎLE DE LA CITÉ & ÎLE SAINT-LOUIS
1ST & 4TH ARRONDISSEMENTS

PARIS BY LOCALS

Explore these islands in the Seine and marvel at the layers of history they embody. Île de la Cité has been the heart of Paris since the *Iron Age*, whereas Île Saint-Louis, the younger of the two islands, was largely developed in the seventeenth century. While *Notre-Dame* is the most visited destination on either island, there is plenty more to *tempt visitors*. Wandering Île Saint-Louis, you could almost imagine you are in a quaint village, with its narrow cobbled streets and charming bistros. And as you explore Île de la Cité, you can sense the *power and authority* that this island once exerted. Before exploring either island, a walk around the perimeter is a great way to get your bearings.

Atelier du Geste à l'Émotion

27 Place Dauphine, 75001, 1st Arr.

A delightful pâtisserie. In nice weather you can enjoy your treats outside in the leafy square.

Deportation Memorial

7 Quai de l'Archevêché, 75004, 4th Arr.

Opened in 1962, this modernist monument commemorates those sent to Nazi concentration camps during World War II.

Notre-Dame Cathedral

6 Parvis Notre-Dame, 75004, 4th Arr.

The spiritual heart of Paris, where kings of France were crowned, the last coronation being that of Napoléon Bonaparte. Completed by 1220, it is the most recognized landmark in Paris. Be sure to walk around the outside of the cathedral as there is a lovely square behind it that is never as crowded as the front.

Pont Neuf

75001, 1st Arr.

Named 'new bridge' when it was built in 1607, this bridge is now the oldest bridge in Paris.

Restaurant Paul

15 Place Dauphine, 75001, 1st Arr.

A charming restaurant serving traditional French fare, looking out onto a delightful public square.

Sainte-Chapelle

10 Blvd du Palais, 75001, 1st Arr.

If you only have time to do one thing on Île de la Cité, visit this thirteenth-century chapel. It is a masterpiece of gothic architecture and has some of the most stunning stained glass in the world.

Square du Vert-Galant
15 Place du Pont Neuf, 75001, 1st Arr.
A quaint garden with lovely views of the Seine.

Île Saint-Louis

Berthillon
31 Rue Saint-Louis en l'Île, 75004, 4th Arr.
Adored by locals and tourists alike, the ice cream here is incredible, and worth the queue in peak season.

La Ferme Saint-Aubin
76 Rue Saint-Louis en l'Île, 75004, 4th Arr.
This fromagerie has a wonderful and vast assortment of French cheeses, where you will be sure to find something new.

Minicafé
1 Rue des Deux Ponts, 75004, 4th Arr.
The name says it all; it's a cute and tiny café serving up great drinks and a small selection of sweet baked goods.

Pâtisserie Tourbillon Saint-Louis
90 Rue Saint-Louis en l'Île, 75004, 4th Arr.
Enjoy pâtisserie created by an award-winning pastry chef, plus handmade chocolates and, at weekends, desserts too.

Square Barye
2 Blvd Henri IV, 75004, 4th Arr.
Located on the easternmost tip of the island, this is a great place to sit and rest your feet, enjoying views of the river while you recharge.

Compagnie Française
des Poivres et
des Epices

Assouline Paris

Debauve &
Gallais

Aux Merveilleux
de Fred

Café de Flore

Breizh
Café

Holy
Cookie

Café Le Procope

Les Deux Magots

Fou de
Pâtisserie

Popelini

Grom

Le Café
Pierre Hermé

The Red
Wheelbarrow

Luxembourg Palace

SAINT-GERMAIN-DES-PRÉS
6TH ARRONDISSEMENT

Known for its *intellectual* and artistic history, this neighbourhood was originally home to a *Benedictine abbey*. The church, Saint-Germain-des-Prés, is one of the *oldest* in Paris, having been rebuilt in the tenth century. In the twentieth century, Saint-Germain-des-Prés became a hub of the French *existentialist* movement. Jean-Paul Sartre and Simone de Beauvoir lived in the neighbourhood, and their work was influenced by the intellectual and *political ferment* of the era. The neighbourhood was also home to Albert Camus, *Pablo Picasso* and Ernest Hemingway. Today, Saint-Germain-des-Prés is still a *popular destination* for tourists and locals alike. The neighbourhood is dotted with cafés, bars and restaurants, as well as *art galleries* and bookstores. It is a vibrant and lively neighbourhood and one to be experienced on a visit to Paris.

Assouline Paris

35 Rue Bonaparte, 75006, 6th Arr.

A luxury bookshop and publisher offering gorgeous books on art, design, fashion and lifestyle.

Aux Merveilleux de Fred

1 Rue de l'Ancienne Comédie, 75006, 6th Arr.

Go for the chocolate brioche, stay for the delicious meringues. (Top tip: get an extra chocolate brioche for future you.)

Breizh Café

1 Rue de l'Odéon, 75006, 6th Arr.

Traditional Breton crêpes and galettes made with sweet or savoury fillings.

Café de Flore

172 Blvd Saint-Germain, 75006, 6th Arr.

Frequented by de Beauvoir, Hemingway, Picasso and Salvador Dalí, this café is popular with tourists but well worth a visit.

Le Café Pierre Hermé

126 Blvd Saint-Germain, 75006, 6th Arr.

Enjoy exquisite macarons, pâtisserie and artisan drinks by iconic chef Pierre Hermé.

Café Le Procope

13 Rue de l'Ancienne Comédie, 75006, 6th Arr.

A timeless institution that has been serving up delicious food and wine for generations.

Compagnie Française des Poivres et des Epices

7 Rue de Furstemberg, 75006, 6th Arr.

One of the fanciest spice shops, which is worth a visit if you love to cook. It is truly one of a kind.

Debauve & Gallais

30 Rue des Saints-Pères, 75007, 6th Arr.

A renowned chocolatier that has been expertly crafting chocolates since 1817.

Les Deux Magots

6 Place Saint-Germain-des-Prés, 75006, 6th Arr.

A stone's throw from Café de Flore, this famous café and restaurant was a meeting place for artists and intellectuals in the early twentieth century. Its charm remains, making it a popular place to visit still.

Fou de Pâtisserie

64 Rue de Seine, 75006, 6th Arr.

An aggregator of pastries from different top-notch French confectioners. Your one-stop shop for trying some of the best pâtisserie in Paris.

Grom

81 Rue de Seine, 75006, 6th Arr.

Here the gelato is freshly made to perfection, using high-quality ingredients, in classic flavours.

Holy Cookie

70 Rue Saint-André des Arts, 75006, 6th Arr.

Generously sized cookies baked with unique flavours and fillings. Go with friends and share.

Luxembourg Palace

15 Rue de Vaugirard, 75006, 6th Arr.

A baroque palace that is now home to the French Senate. You can take a tour of the inside on days when the Senate is not in session.

Popelini

47 Rue du Cherche-Midi, 75006, 6th Arr.

Delicious choux-filled pastries that are flavoured to perfection. They make the most delightful little snack.

The Red Wheelbarrow

9/11 Rue de Médicis, 75006, 6th Arr.

More relaxed and much less crowded than other English bookshops in Paris, but with a wonderful selection of carefully curated books.

Cuppa
Gallery

Deyrolle

BONTON

BARTHÉLÉMY

Bonton

Chocolat
Chapon

Maillol
Museum

Barthélémy

Rodin
Museum

Angelina

THE
CONRAN
SHOP

HUGO & VICTOR

L'Appartement Sézane

The
Conran Shop

Hugo & Victor

Square
Boucicaut

LA GRANDE ÉPICERIE DE PARIS

LE BON MARCHÉ

La Grande
Épicerie de Paris

Le Bon
Marché

RUE DU BAC
7TH ARRONDISSEMENT

This charming corner of the 7th arrondissement is full of *delightful* shops, fascinating museums, delicious cafés and quaint garden squares. With its *elegant* architecture and ambience, it is quite easy to while away an afternoon here *window shopping*, people-watching and sauntering. The relaxed yet *sophisticated* atmosphere, helped by the seventeenth- and eighteenth-century *architecture*, makes this a popular destination for Parisians as well as tourists.

Angelina
108 Rue du Bac, 75007, 7th Arr.
This iconic Parisian pâtisserie has delicious desserts and the most decadent hot chocolate.

L'Appartement Sézane
122 Rue du Bac, 75007, 7th Arr.
This women's clothing store stocks wonderful styles that perfectly capture French chic.

Barthélémy
51 Rue de Grenelle, 75007, 7th Arr.
Founded in 1921, this fromagerie exudes a certain vintage charm alongside an amazing offering of French cheeses.

Le Bon Marché
24 Rue de Sèvres, 75007, 7th Arr.
Open since 1838, this is one of the oldest department stores in the world. Offering high-end fashion and homeware, it is a wonderful place to spend some time browsing.

Bonton
82 Rue de Grenelle, 75007, 7th Arr.
A delightful kids' clothing and toy shop with a superb curation of accessories and outfits.

Chocolat Chapon
69 Rue du Bac, 75007, 7th Arr.
Pick your chocolate based on the country of origin and flavour undertones, and be sure to try the chocolate mousse.

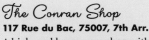

The Conran Shop
117 Rue du Bac, 75007, 7th Arr.
A high-end homeware shop with a great selection of furniture, lighting, accessories and more from renowned designers.

Cuppa Gallery
86 Rue de l'Université, 75007, 7th Arr.
A small and delightful café serving up a small selection of dishes and warm drinks.

Deyrolle
46 Rue du Bac, 75007, 7th Arr.
In operation since 1831, this taxidermy shop and museum is a true curiosity. They sell gardening and gift items alongside stuffed exotic animals.

La Grande Épicerie de Paris
38 Rue de Sèvres, 75007, 7th Arr.
This luxury food hall offers a wonderful assortment of gourmet products from around the world.

Hugo & Victor
40 Blvd Raspail, 75007, 7th Arr.
A delightful pâtisserie with a wonderful assortment of cakes and treats.

Maillol Museum
59–61 Rue de Grenelle, 75007, 7th Arr.
Featuring over 600 pieces from Aristide Maillol, the renowned French sculptor who reinvented modern sculpture.

Rodin Museum
77 Rue de Varenne, 75007, 7th Arr.
Former home turned museum dedicated to the works of the sculptor Auguste Rodin. Some of Rodin's most famous works, such as *The Thinker*, *The Kiss* and *The Gates of Hell*, are on display at the museum and its adjoining garden.

Square Boucicaut
1 Rue de Babylone, 75007, 7th Arr.
This park is a great place to rest and it features a charming tiny carousel.

Le 975

La Maison Rose

Arnaud Larher

Montmartre Museum

Vigne du Clos Montmartre

Montmartre Cemetery

Maison Aleph

Photobooth

Dalí Museum

Sacré-Coeur

The Hardware Société

La Bossue

Pâtisserie Gilles Marchal

L'Objet qui Parle

Boris Lumé Café Pâtisserie

Bouillon Pigalle

MONTMARTRE
18TH ARRONDISSEMENT

PARIS BY LOCALS

Crowned by the Basilica of the *Sacred Heart* (Sacré-Coeur), Montmartre has a long and rich history. Over the centuries this *hill* has been a Benedictine abbey, a pilgrimage site, a vineyard, an *artistic commune* and the centre of *bohemian* life in the city. Here history, art and culture meet in charming streets filled with cafés, galleries and museums. Top tip: start at the top for *stunning vistas* of Paris; it is quite a big hill and much easier to enjoy the view while *ambling down* than while walking up.

Arnaud Larher
53 Rue Caulaincourt, 75018, 18th Arr.
Selling a wonderful assortment of handcrafted chocolates, desserts, and macarons. Grab an éclair or dessert to eat right away, and some chocolate to enjoy later.

Boris Lumé Café Pâtisserie
28 Rue Lepic, 75018, 18th Arr.
Coffee shop and pâtisserie that is the perfect place to stop for an afternoon pick-me-up.

La Bossue
9 Rue Joseph de Maistre, 75018, 18th Arr.
Enjoy a delightful meal at this charming neighbourhood bakery.

Bouillon Pigalle
22 Blvd de Clichy, 75018, 18th Arr.
A modern brasserie serving up classic French dishes at very reasonable prices.

Dalí Museum
11 Rue Poulbot, 75018, 18th Arr.
Celebrating the work of the Surrealist artist, this museum houses over 300 original pieces of art including paintings, sculptures, and drawings.

The Hardware Société
10 Rue Lamarck, 75018, 18th Arr.
Serving up Aussie-style breakfast and brunch in a charming location with views of Paris rooftops.

Maison Aleph
63 Rue des Abbesses, 75018, 18th Arr.
A hot chocolate not to be missed; add any of the delicious pastries on offer for the perfect combo.

La Maison Rose
2 Rue de l'Abreuvoir, 75018, 18th Arr.
This iconic pink restaurant in Montmartre has been a local favourite since the 1850s.

Montmartre Cemetery
20 Avenue Rachel, 75018, 18th Arr.

This cemetery is the final resting place of many artists and writers, including Degas and Zola.

Montmartre Museum
12 Rue Cortot, 75018, 18th Arr.

This museum explores the history and culture of Montmartre from the nineteenth century onwards and was once home to the Impressionist painter Renoir. Explore the gardens with views of the last vineyard in Paris.

Le 975
185 Rue Marcadet, 75018, 18th Arr.

Creative, seasonal cuisine enjoyed in a pared-down, friendly atmosphere.

L'Objet qui Parle
86 Rue des Martyrs, 75018, 18th Arr.

A wonderfully curated antique shop selling a wide array of curiosities and vintage objects.

Pâtisserie Gilles Marchal
9 Rue Ravignan, 75018, 18th Arr.

Decisions, decisions ... when everything looks this good, you can't get it wrong.

Photobooth
53 Rue des Trois Frères, 18th Arr.

A traditional photobooth with black and white photos, a perfect souvenir from Paris.

Sacré-Coeur
35 Rue du Chevalier de la Barre, 75018, 18th Arr.

Built on the highest point in Paris, this Catholic church offers sweeping views of the city.

Vigne du Clos Montmartre
18 Rue des Saules, 75018, 18th Arr.

Dating to the twelfth century, this vineyard has remained a cornerstone that ties the area to its village roots.

Place de la Concorde

Musée de l'Orangerie

Tuileries Garden

Louvre

Bookstall Quays of Paris

Eiffel Tower

Hôtel des Invalides

Musée d'Orsay

Saint-Michel Fountain

Notre-Dame Cathedral

THE SEINE

Walking along the Seine is a wonderful way to experience
Paris. As the *river winds* through the city, you'll discover
iconic landmarks, palaces and gardens. Around each bend
of the approximately five-kilometre path that cuts through
the heart of Paris, thousands of years of the *city's history*
unfolds before you. The left bank offers up scenic views of the
buildings across the river, while the right bank is lined with
outdoor cafés and has a slightly slower pace. This walk is
the perfect time to be a *flâneur*, a wanderer and observer of
city life. The riverside is bookended by the Eiffel Tower and
Notre-Dame, both ideal places to start or finish a walk.

Bookstall Quays of Paris

6 Quai de la Mégisserie, 75001, 1st Arr.

There is a certain excitement to browsing the second-hand bookstalls nestled along the Seine, with their seemingly endless rows of old books, maps and prints. There are hidden treasures to be found in each one.

Eiffel Tower

Champ de Mars, 5 Avenue Anatole France, 75007, 7th Arr.

Enjoy a crêpe from one of the many vendors selling them around the Eiffel Tower – a great way to start or end a walk.

Hôtel des Invalides

129 Rue de Grenelle, 75007, 7th Arr.

This gold-domed building houses a museum of French military history as well as the tomb of Napoléon Bonaparte.

Louvre

75001, 1st Arr.

This former royal palace, which was home to the French royal family for centuries, is now one of the largest museums in the world. The original palace was built in the twelfth century and its ruins can be seen in the basement of the Louvre. The current palace was built in the seventeenth century, and today houses a vast collection of art and antiquities from around the world.

Musée de l'Orangerie

Jardin des Tuileries, 75001, 1st Arr.

Monet's curved waterlily paintings were specially created for the museum. Having the artworks surround you immerses you right into the paintings and is a must-see.

Musée d'Orsay

Esplanade Valéry Giscard d'Estaing, 75007, 7th Arr.
Incontestably *the* Impressionist museum,
its collection includes works by some of the
most famous artists of the Impressionist and
Post-Impressionist movements.

Notre-Dame Cathedral
6 Parvis Notre-Dame, 75004, 4th Arr.
Taking nearly 200 years to build, this gothic architectural masterpiece
was completed in 1345. It was here that kings and emperors of France were
crowned and is one of the most recognized landmarks in Paris.

Place de la Concorde
75008, 8th Arr.
Used for public executions during the French Revolution, this square is
now home to the Luxor Obelisk and two ornate fountains.

Saint-Michel Fountain
Place Saint-Michel, 75005, 5th Arr.
Depicting the Archangel Michael vanquishing the Devil, this epic bronze
and marble fountain is a reminder of the city's rich history and its strong
commitment to the arts.

Tuileries Garden
Place de la Concorde, 75001, 1st Arr.
Iconic tree-lined garden filled with statues – and chairs for relaxing and
enjoying the atmosphere.

Galeries
Lafayette

Ici Librairie

Printemps

Café Nuances

Palais Garnier

Momzi
Donuts

BNF Richelieu

Immersion
Vendôme

Café de la Paix

Galeri
Colbert

Danico

OPÉRA

2ND & 9TH ARRONDISSEMENTS

PARIS BY LOCALS

Home to a number of *luxury hotels*, restaurants and shops, Opéra is an area full of historic *opulence*. Its name comes from the centrepiece of this neighbourhood, the Palais Garnier (home of the city's *ballet and opera* companies), and you can easily feel as if you have stepped back into *nineteenth-century* Paris. With enclosed shopping galleries, quaint cafés and *truly spectacular* architecture, this is an area well worth exploring.

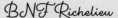

BNF Richelieu
58 Rue de Richelieu, 75002, 2nd Arr.
One of two main sites for the National Library of France, this library and museum houses an amazing collection of books and manuscripts.

Café de la Paix
5 Place de l'Opéra, 75009, 9th Arr.
This opulent café offers front-row seats to the Palais Garnier. An ideal place to enjoy a meal or an afternoon snack while also enjoying the view.

Café Nuances
25 Rue Danielle Casanova, 75001, 1st Arr.
Passionate about the perfect coffee with distinctive coffees from around the world.

Danico
6 Rue Vivienne, 75002, 2nd Arr.
Located at the back of Daroco restaurant you will find this cosy cocktail bar serving up original drinks.

Galerie Colbert
1 Passage Colbert, 75002, 2nd Arr.
This immaculate arcade features a wonderful assortment of shops, as well as a few restaurants and cafés.

Galeries Lafayette
40 Blvd Haussmann, 75009, 9th Arr.
One of the most famous department stores in the city, with a glass dome designed by Gustave Eiffel. A visit is as much about seeing the building as going shopping. Head to the top floor for views over Paris.

Ici Librairie
25 Blvd Poissonnière, 75002, 2nd Arr.
The largest independent bookstore in Paris, this is a wonderful place to explore with a wide selection of books in French (and some in English too). It also has a café, making it a great place to relax and read.

Immersion Vendôme
23 Rue Danielle Casanova, 75001, 1st Arr.
From sweet to savoury, this café offers something for everyone.

Momzi Donuts
1 Rue Cherubini, 75002, 2nd Arr.
Doughnut concept bakery with a Parisian twist. Serving unique and innovative flavours, it is a great place to try something new.

Palais Garnier
Place de l'Opéra, 75009, 9th Arr.
A masterpiece of beaux-arts architecture, this opera house boasts a ceiling painted by Chagall as well as lavish gold leaf, marble and crystal décor. It may be better known for its role in Gaston Leroux's novel *The Phantom of the Opera*!

Printemps
64 Blvd Haussmann, 75009, 9th Arr.
Another famous department store, which is not usually as crowded as others, but has an equally impressive selection of clothing, homeware and more. It also boasts rooftop bars and restaurants with stunning views of Paris.

Ellsworth

Juveniles

Aki Boulangerie

La Droguerie

Ritz Paris

Le Soufflé

Angelina

Astier de Villatte

Bistrot Mee

Palais Royal

Bourse de Commerce

Cédric Grolet

Librairie Galignani

Kodawari Ramen

Louvre

Clover Grill

Museum of Decorative Arts

LOUVRE
1ST ARRONDISSEMENT

One of the *smallest* and most historic districts of Paris,
the 1st arrondissement is located on the right bank of
the Seine. Its location has made it a major centre for
commerce and culture since the first palace was built
here in the Middle Ages. Home to this area's namesake,
the Louvre, one of the *biggest museums* in the world, this
part of the city can understandably get very busy, but
a street or two away from the main thoroughfares
will take you to more *tranquil areas.*

Aki Boulangerie
16 Rue Sainte-Anne, 75001, 1st Arr.
A delightful Japanese bakery in the heart of Paris. Try the melon bread or the black sesame éclair.

Angelina
226 Rue de Rivoli, 75001, 1st Arr.
This iconic pâtisserie has delicious desserts and decadent hot chocolate.

Astier de Villatte
173 Rue Saint-Honoré, 75001, 1st Arr.
Truly unique ceramics and items for the home. Expertly handcrafted modern pieces with a vintage feel.

Ritz Paris
15 Place Vendôme, 75001, 1st Arr.
While most of us can't afford to stay the night at the Ritz, we can enjoy the cafés and bars. For desserts stop by Ritz Paris Le Comptoir, enjoy drinks in Bar Hemingway or have afternoon tea in the Salon Proust.

Bistrot Mee
5 Rue d'Argenteuil, 75001, 1st Arr.
A great Korean restaurant with tasty dishes served in a cosy atmosphere. If in doubt, go for the bibimbap.

Bourse de Commerce
2 Rue de Viarmes, 75001, 1st Arr.
One of the newer museums in Paris, the Bourse de Commerce houses the Pinault Collection of over 10,000 works of contemporary art.

Clover Grill
6 Rue Bailleul, 75001, 1st Arr.
A truly great steak restaurant with the finest cuts cooked to perfection.

La Droguerie
9–11 Rue du Jour, 75001, 1st Arr.
A delightful haberdashery with an amazing selection of ribbons, binding, detailing from feathers to flowers, and more. A must for the craft lover.

Ellsworth
34 Rue de Richelieu, 75001, 1st Arr.
Intimate restaurant with à la carte and set menus featuring classic dishes.

Juveniles
47 Rue de Richelieu, 75001, 1st Arr.
A charming bistro serving French comfort food and delightful desserts.

Kodawari Ramen
12 Rue de Richelieu, 75001, 1st Arr.
Traditional Japanese ramen served in this quaint restaurant where the fresh fish is on display.

Librairie Galignani
224 Rue de Rivoli, 75001, 1st Arr.
Located in a historic setting just across from the Tuileries Garden, this beautiful bookstore has a wide selection of books in English and French.

Louvre
75001, 1st Arr.
This vast museum is a true labyrinth with treasures around every corner.

Museum of Decorative Arts
107 Rue de Rivoli, 75001, 1st Arr.
An expansive collection covering from the Middle Ages to the present day.

Palais-Royal
Place Colette, 75001, 1st Arr.
Enjoy the iconic striped columns in the gardens followed by a delicious drink and pastry from Café Kitsuné.

La Pâtisserie du Meurice Cédric Grolet
6 Rue de Castiglione, 75001, 1st Arr.
The world-renowned pastry chef is known for his creative desserts.

Le Soufflé
36 Rue du Mont Thabor, 75001, 1st Arr.
Sweet and savoury soufflés can be enjoyed in this charming restaurant.

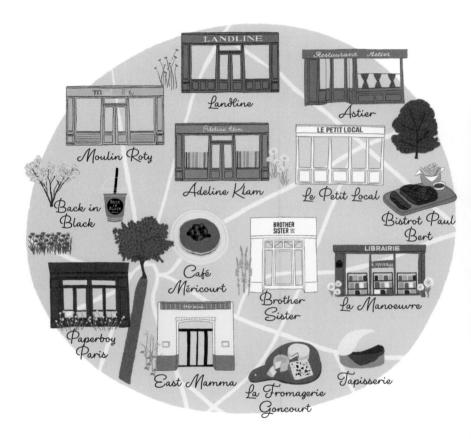

Moulin Roty

Landline

Astier

Back in Black

Adeline Klam

Le Petit Local

Bistrot Paul Bert

Café Méricourt

Brother Sister

La Manoeuvre

Paperboy Paris

East Mamma

La Fromagerie Goncourt

Tapisserie

BASTILLE
11ᵀᴴ ARRONDISSEMENT

PARIS BY LOCALS

If you want to avoid the more touristy areas of Paris, head to the 11th for *vibrant and eclectic* restaurants and cafés, cool independent shops and a more relaxed atmosphere. You can experience the best of Paris here. This area has been *transformed* time and time again since it was first developed in the Middle Ages. At the heart is *Bastille,* a large square where the Bastille prison once stood. The storming of the Bastille began the *French Revolution* and today the square is used as a meeting place as well as a place of protest.

Adeline Klam
54 Blvd Richard-Lenoir, 75011, 11th Arr.
This craft shop sells the most vibrant Japanese papers and textiles, as well as a small selection of charming homeware and gifts.

Astier
44 Rue Jean-Pierre Timbaud, 75011, 11th Arr.
Classic French bistro that has been serving up French staples since 1956.

Back in Black
25 Rue Amelot, 75011, 11th Arr.
Excellent range of handcrafted coffee and great brunch options as well.

Bistrot Paul Bert
18 Rue Paul Bert, 75011, 11th Arr.
Quintessential Parisian bistro serving up classics such as steaks, soufflés and scallops.

Brother Sister
72 Rue de la Roquette, 75011, 11th Arr.
American-style brunch staples in a delightful setting.

Café Méricourt
22 Rue de la Folie Méricourt, 75011, 11th Arr.
A great spot to grab brunch, with both sweet and savoury options. From shakshuka to pancakes, granola to perfectly made drinks.

East Mamma
133 Rue du Faubourg Saint-Antoine, 75011, 11th Arr.
This vibrant Italian restaurant serves up classic Italian dishes cooked to perfection. Be sure to save room for the chocolate mousse.

La Fromagerie Goncourt
1 Rue Abel Rabaud, 75011, 11th Arr.

An excellent variety of cheeses is available here, with passionate staff who will go above and beyond to explain and help you find the perfect cheese.

Landline
107 Avenue Parmentier, 75011, 11th Arr.

Everyday goods for the home and gifts of the highest quality, sourced from across France.

La Manoeuvre
58 Rue de la Roquette, 75011, 11th Arr.

A neighbourhood favourite boasting a wide selection of books, it is the perfect place to spend an afternoon browsing the shelves.

Moulin Roty
22 Blvd des Filles du Calvaire, 75011, 11th Arr.

This colourful shop is full of toys designed for curious children who love to explore.

Paperboy Paris
137 Rue Amelot, 75011, 11th Arr.

A delightful brunch spot – my recommendation is the pain perdu (otherwise known as French toast).

Le Petit Local
51 Rue du Chemin Vert, 75011, 11th Arr.

A magnificent little shop selling games and toys for children of all ages.

Tapisserie
65 Rue de Charonne, 75011, 11th Arr.

A petite pâtisserie whisking up incredible flans, tarts, choux and more.

Fondation
Louis Vuitton

Korean
Garden

Jardin
d'Acclimatation

Château de Bagatelle

Lac
Inférieur

Shakespeare
Garden

Jardin des
Serres d'Auteuil

Musée Marmottan
Monet

BOIS DE BOULOGNE
16TH ARRONDISSEMENT

PARIS BY LOCALS

This *beautiful and historic* park started as a royal hunting ground in the Middle Ages. The nineteenth century saw it transformed into a public park, designed in the English landscape style with *winding paths*, lakes and forests. It was here that the Duke and Duchess of Windsor made a home for themselves after leaving Britain, in a house that is now open to the public. As well as its *royal history* it also hosts the *French Open* tennis tournament at Roland Garros Stadium. Today, it is a popular place to relax and enjoy the outdoors, feeling a world away from the hustle and bustle of Paris.

Château de Bagatelle
35 Route de Sèvres à Neuilly, 75016, 16th Arr.
Built for Louis XVI's brother, this small château with beautiful gardens was a favourite place for the aristocracy to escape Paris and enjoy what was then country air.

Fondation Louis Vuitton
8 Avenue du Mahatma Gandhi, 75116, 16th Arr.
This striking building by Frank Gehry houses a wonderful collection of contemporary art.

Jardin d'Acclimatation
Bois de Boulogne, 75116, 16th Arr.
The first amusement park in France is still a firm favourite with children and families today. With delightful rides, a petting zoo and boating lake, it is a great place to enjoy a day out.

Korean Garden
Bois de Boulogne, 75116, 16th Arr.
A beautifully landscaped traditional Korean garden located inside the Jardin d'Acclimatation.

Lac Inférieur
Bois de Boulogne, 75016, 16th Arr.
Hire a boat and paddle around this small lake near the lawns of Muette to take in the beautiful scenery.

Musée Marmottan Monet
2 Rue Louis Boilly, 75016, 16th Arr.
This small museum is home to over 300 paintings by Monet as well as paintings from his personal collection. It is the largest collection of his work in one place. (He painted around 2,000 works in his lifetime.)

Shakespeare Garden
Bois de Boulogne, 75016, 16th Arr.
A beautiful, quiet and peaceful garden that is the perfect place to take a leisurely stroll.

Jardin des Serres d'Auteuil
3 Avenue de la Porte d'Auteuil, 75016, 16th Arr.
The first botanical garden was created here in 1761 under Louis XV and the gardens have been added to ever since. Exploring the impressive glass houses, featuring exotic plants from around the world, is a wonderful way to pass an afternoon.

PARIS

BY INTEREST

PART THREE

IMPRESSIONIST PARIS + REVOLUTIONARY PARIS + LITERARY PARIS

+ CYCLING PARIS + CASTLES & PALACES + CHARMING STREETS

+ BEST VIEWS + CHILDREN'S PARIS + MUSEUMS + BOOKSTORES

Montmartre
Cemetery

Le Consulat

La Maison Rose

Musée
Marmottan
Monet

Musée de
Montmartre

Musée
de l'Orangerie

The Seine &
Tuileries Garden

Musée
d'Orsay

Musée
Fournaise

further out

Café de Flore

Fondation
Monet

IMPRESSIONIST PARIS

Paris was the epicentre of the *Impressionist art* movement, drawing young artists to its streets with its *intellectual climate*, diverse population and beautiful vistas. Eschewing their classical roots, young artists such as Claude Monet, Edgar Degas, Pierre-Auguste Renoir and Camille Pissarro created a *new approach* to painting that was centred on capturing the fleeting effects of light and atmosphere. These artists found *inspiration* in the world around them, painting the diversity reflected in the city from the wealthy to the working class. Their paintings captured the *energy* and movement of Paris, and their work continues to inspire artists and *art lovers* alike.

Café de Flore
172 Blvd Saint-Germain, 75006, 6th Arr.

Although no longer the intellectual and Impressionist hotspot it was in the 19th century, the history of this café makes it worth a visit. Enjoy a hot chocolate and the atmosphere.

Le Consulat
18 Rue Norvins, 75018, 18th Arr.

A historic café in Montmartre that was once frequented by artists such as Pablo Picasso, Vincent van Gogh, Alfred Sisley, Narcisse Virgilio Díaz and Henri de Toulouse-Lautrec. There's outdoor seating on a charming, cobbled lane.

Fondation Monet
84 Rue Claude Monet, 27620, Giverny (open from April to November)

Two and a half hours outside Paris is Monet's former home and garden, which has been turned into a museum. Exploring the grounds feels like you are stepping right into a Monet painting.

La Maison Rose
2 Rue de l'Abreuvoir, 75018, 18th Arr.

This iconic pink restaurant in Montmartre has been a local favourite since the 1850s. It was a frequented by Impressionist painters who lived and worked in the area.

Montmartre Cemetery
20 Avenue Rachel, 75018, 18th Arr.

This cemetery is the final resting place of many artists and writers, including Degas.

Musée Fournaise
3 Rue du Bac, 78400, Chatou

Located on the idyllic Île de Chatou, a popular spot for Impressionists to meet and paint. Renoir painted *en plein air* here and you can stroll along the island's Impressionist trail to learn more about its history.

Musée de l'Orangerie

Jardin des Tuileries, 75001, 1st Arr.

Monet's curved waterlily paintings were specially created for the museum. Having the artworks surround you immerses you right into the paintings and is a must-see.

Musée d'Orsay

Esplanade Valéry Giscard d'Estaing, 75007, 7th Arr.

Incontestably *the* Impressionist museum, its collection includes works by some of the most famous artists of the Impressionist and Post-Impressionist movements, including Monet, Édouard Manet, Degas, Renoir, Paul Cézanne, Van Gogh and Paul Gauguin.

Musée de Montmartre

12 Rue Cortot, 75018, 18th Arr.

This museum explores the history and culture of Montmartre from the 19th century onwards and was once home to Renoir. Explore the gardens with views of the last vineyard in Paris.

Musée Marmottan Monet

2 Rue Louis Boilly, 75016, 16th Arr.

This small museum is home to over 300 paintings by Monet as well as paintings from his personal collection. It is the largest collection of his work in one place.

The Seine & Tuileries Garden

Place de la Concorde, 75001, 1st Arr.

One of the best ways to walk in the footsteps of the Impressionists is to stroll down the streets they painted, sit in the gardens they immortalized in their paintings, and embrace the energy and movement of the city. A walk along the River Seine or through the Tuileries Garden is a great place to start.

Palais-Royal

Louvre

Hôtel de Ville

Place de la Concorde

Conciergerie

Bastille

Pont de la Concorde

Notre-Dame Cathedral

Les Invalides

Picpus Cemetery

Cour du Commerce Saint-André

Palace of Versailles

Panthéon

Luxembourg Palace

REVOLUTIONARY PARIS

PARIS BY INTEREST

The city of Paris was at the heart of the *French Revolution*. In July 1789 the storming of the Bastille, a prison seen as a symbol of *royal* authority, started a chain of events that ultimately led to the eventual abolition of the *monarchy* years later.

During the Revolution the population of Paris grew as people from all over the country were drawn to the city to participate, thus changing the demographics and *political landscape* as new institutions emerged. The Revolution was not seamless, and many iterations of government and correlating institutions were created over the years in an attempt to find a new balance that represented the will of the people.

Bastille
Place de la Bastille, 75004, 4th Arr.
The storming of the Bastille on 14 July 1789 kick-started the French Revolution. The July Column now marks its location.

Conciergerie
2 Blvd du Palais, 75001, 1st Arr.
This 14th-century palace became a prison during the Revolution, the most famous inmate being Queen Marie-Antoinette. Today it is a museum and monument with exhibits about the French Revolution.

Cour du Commerce Saint-André
75006, 6th Arr.
This quaint walkway is full of Revolutionary history. There is Le Procope, a café favoured by anti-monarchists. Further along, Joseph Guillotin tested (on sheep) his deathly invention and next door Jean-Paul Marat opened editorial offices for the revolutionary newspaper *L'Ami du Peuple*.

Hôtel de Ville
Place de l'Hôtel-de-Ville, 75004, 4th Arr.
This grand town hall has been used as government offices since 1357. It also served as headquarters for the French Revolution.

Les Invalides
75007, 7th Arr.
Revolutionaries plundered this military hospital, taking 30,000 muskets to attack the Bastille. Today it is a museum and houses the tomb of Napoléon.

Louvre
75001, 1st Arr.
The Louvre was headquarters for the Committee of Public Safety, a provisional government and war cabinet, which oversaw the trials and executions during the Reign of Terror, sentencing thousands of (mostly innocent) people to death by guillotine.

Luxembourg Palace
15 Rue de Vaugirard, 75006, 6th Arr.
Now home to the French Senate, this former royal residence was transformed into a prison during the Revolution.

Notre-Dame Cathedral

6 Parvis Notre-Dame, 75004, 4th Arr.

Dozens of churches, including Notre-Dame, were turned into 'Temples of Reason' as dechristianization unfolded during the Revolution. Twenty-eight statues depicting the Kings of Judea were pulled from the west façade of the cathedral and guillotined in front of the church.

Palace of Versailles

Place d'Armes, 78000, Versailles

Versailles was, and still is, the epitome of opulence and baroque style. In the 18th century, it stood in stark juxtaposition to the starving population.

Palais-Royal

Place Colette, 75001, 1st Arr.

The Palace's arcades became a major centre of Revolutionary activity. In July 1789, a speech by Camille Desmoulins sparked the storming of the Bastille.

Panthéon

Place du Panthéon, 75005, 5th Arr.

In 1791 the building, intended as a church, was turned into a mausoleum. Important French figures are buried here including Voltaire, Jean-Jacques Rousseau, Alexandre Dumas, Émile Zola, Victor Hugo and Marie Curie.

Picpus Cemetery

35 Rue de Picpus, 75012, 12th Arr.

The final resting place of 1,306 headless bodies who lost their lives at the guillotine. Nearly all were condemned for petty, absurd or imaginary crimes.

Place de la Concorde

75008, 8th Arr.

A guillotine replaced a statue of King Louis XV on this square. Many notable people were executed here, including Louis XV's grandson, Marie-Antoinette, Maximilien Robespierre and Camille Desmoulins.

Pont de la Concorde

75007, 7th Arr.

This bridge was partly built using the stones from the Bastille prison as a reminder that the citizens could always trample the monarchy into ruins.

Bar
Hemingway

Émile Zola
Apartment

Balzac
House

BNF Richelieu

Père Lachaise
Cemetery

Victor Hugo
House

L'Hôtel

Hôtel La
Louisiane

Panthéon

Les Deux Magots
and Café de Flore

Gertrude Stein
Salon

Hôtel Luxembourg
Parc

Ernest Hemingway/
James Joyce Apartment

LITERARY PARIS

Paris has a long and rich *literary heritage*. The city has been home to some of the most important writers in *French history*, including Voltaire, Hugo and Marcel Proust. In the 20th century, *Paris* continued to be a major literary centre with resident writers such as Simone de Beauvoir and Jean-Paul Sartre, while also being the epicentre of the *Lost Generation*, a group of expatriate writers and artists who came to the city to escape the *constraints* of their home countries. Some of the most famous members were Ernest Hemingway, F. Scott Fitzgerald and Gertrude Stein. Paris remains a *magnet for writers* from all over the world, drawn to its rich cultural heritage and vibrant intellectual life.

Balzac House
47 Rue Raynouard, 75016, 16th Arr.
Former home of Honoré de Balzac, author of *Le Père Goriot* and *La Cousine Bette*, the residence has been transformed into a museum celebrating his life and his work.

Bar Hemingway
38 Rue Cambon, 75001, 1st Arr.
Located in the Ritz Paris hotel, this bar was 'liberated' by Hemingway while he was embedded as a war correspondent during World War II.

BNF Richelieu
58 Rue de Richelieu, 75002, 2nd Arr.
Part of the National Library of France, this is home to literary treasures including a statue of Voltaire in which his heart is interred.

Les Deux Magots and Café de Flore
6 Place Saint-Germain-des-Prés and 172 Blvd Saint-Germain, 75006, 6th Arr.
Located on adjacent corners, these two cafés were the stomping grounds for artists and intellectuals in the late 19th and early 20th centuries. The likes of Ernest Hemingway, Jean-Paul Sartre, Simone de Beauvoir and many others whiled away the hours here.

Émile Zola Apartment
21 Rue de Bruxelles, 75009, 9th Arr.
A plaque here commemorates the former home of Émile Zola, the French novelist, journalist and playwright. Considered the most prominent French novelist of the late 19th century, he was also a political activist.

Ernest Hemingway Apartment / James Joyce Apartment
714 and 74 Rue du Cardinal Lemoine, 75005, 5th Arr.
Located within 100 metres of each other are the Paris apartments of Hemingway and Joyce, who were drinking companions and offered each other literary support during their time in Paris.

Gertrude Stein Salon
27 Rue de Fleurus, 75006, 6th Arr.
A novelist, poet and playwright, Stein lived in Paris for most of her life and hosted a salon that included notable figures in the literary and art worlds.

L'Hôtel

13 Rue des Beaux Arts, 75006, 6th Arr.

Although a celebrated writer today, Oscar Wilde died in poverty at this hotel in 1900. The hotel celebrates its most notorious guest and even has a cocktail bar named after him.

Hôtel La Louisiane

60 Rue de Seine, 75006, 6th Arr.

Simone de Beauvoir, groundbreaking thinker and writer who challenged traditional gender roles and expectations, lived at this hotel. Her book *The Second Sex* is considered a foundation text of modern feminism.

Hôtel Luxembourg Parc

42 Rue de Vaugirard, 75006, 6th Arr.

William Faulkner, like many American writers in the early 20th century, spent time in Paris, embracing the bohemian environment and letting the city influence his writing. His former home is now the hotel.

Panthéon

Place du Panthéon, 75005, 5th Arr.

This secular mausoleum is the final resting place of some of France's most notable writers, including Voltaire, Rousseau and Victor Hugo.

Père Lachaise Cemetery

75020, 20th Arr.

At Père Lachaise you'll find the graves of literary greats such as Oscar Wilde, Gertrude Stein, Molière, Marcel Proust and many more, including Jim Morrison of The Doors.

Victor Hugo House

6 Place des Vosges, 75004, 4th Arr.

One of the most celebrated French writers, Hugo's most famous works include *The Hunchback of Notre-Dame* and *Les Misérables*. He was also a political activist and politician who was exiled for 20 years when Napoléon III proclaimed himself Emperor of France.

Bois de
Boulogne

Canal
Saint-Martin

Bois de
Vincennes

Seine River

Palace of
Versailles

CYCLING PARIS

One of the best ways to *experience* Paris is by bike, and the city boasts some lovely dedicated cycleways offering up *scenic views*. With miles of paths to choose from, you can easily enjoy a long solo ride, a *short ride* with friends or make an entire day out of it. From enjoying a quiet pedal through a *park* to scenic rides along the *Seine*, these cycle paths make a fun and *unique way* to explore Paris. Don't worry if you don't have a bike; rentals are *easily available* from docking stations across the city.

Seine River

The Left Bank: Undoubtably the most scenic ride in Paris. Start at Pont de l'Archevêché and follow the left bank of the river enjoying the views of Notre-Dame, the Louvre, the Tuileries Garden and Musée d'Orsay before ending your ride at the Eiffel Tower. Before you head off consider stopping at A. Lacroix Pâtissier for a hot drink or delicious pastry.

The Right Bank: The pedestrianized right bank of the river is a great option if you are cycling with kids. Start your ride at Pont de Sully and finish at Tuileries Garden. The path is lined with outdoor cafés and the pace is slower than on the left bank, giving you ample time to soak in the ambience of the city or stop for a drink.

Bois de Boulogne

75016, 16th Arr.

This large park is located to the west of Paris. It's a great place to go for a bike ride, as there are plenty of paths to explore. You can also stop to visit the park's many attractions, such as the Jardin d'Acclimatation (which has activities for children), Fondation Louis Vuitton, Château de Bagatelle or one of the beautiful landscaped gardens.

Bois de Vincennes

75012, 12th Arr.

Another sizeable park, to the east of Paris, and a fantastic option for a day on two wheels. The park contains four artificial lakes and many other features worth stopping for, such as the Château de Vincennes, floral park and the Vincennes Woods.

Canal Saint-Martin

75010, 10th Arr.

This canal is a popular spot for Parisians to relax and enjoy the outdoors, and it's a great place to cycle. Start this ride at the southernmost end of Canal Saint-Martin and follow the cycle path north. Bike along the canal until you reach La Villette, which has a handful of bars and restaurants.

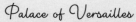

Palace of Versailles

This famous baroque palace is located just outside Paris. While you can't cycle in the formal gardens of the palace, its park is a wonderful place to explore by bike. The expansive grounds with stunning views of the estate and glimpses of the palace can be visited at your leisure. Bike rentals are available at the gardens.

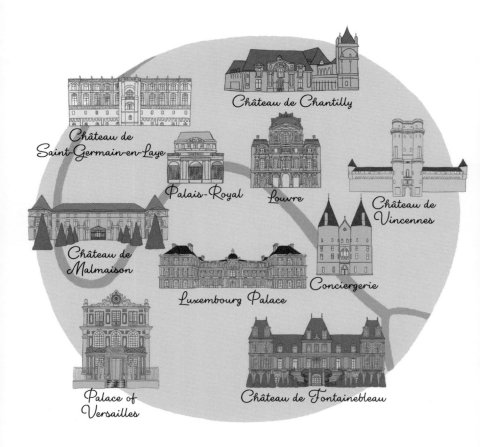

Château de Chantilly

Château de
Saint-Germain-en-Laye

Palais-Royal

Louvre

Château de
Vincennes

Château de
Malmaison

Luxembourg Palace

Conciergerie

Palace of
Versailles

Château de Fontainebleau

CASTLES & PALACES

The châteaux in and around Paris date back to the 12th century. Spanning almost every style, size and design, these *royal residences* offer a glimpse into the lives of the rulers of France. From around the *14th century*, the French monarchy began to build grand châteaux around Paris. These *castles* served as royal residences as well as symbols of their power and *prestige*. Although the French *Revolution* brought an end to the monarchy, many of these castles have survived, *transformed* and evolved. The *history* that is enshrined in them can be experienced by spending a day exploring these castles, museums, gardens and grounds.

Château de Chantilly

60500, Chantilly

This chateau is located about 45 kilometres north of Paris. It was built in the 16th century and is now home to the Condé, a fine art museum. The château has beautiful gardens designed by André Le Nôtre that include a large lake, a maze and a number of fountains.

Château de Fontainebleau

77300, Fontainebleau

A UNESCO World Heritage Site located about 50 kilometres south west of Paris. It was the home of 34 French kings and two emperors from the 12th to the 19th centuries.

Château de Malmaison

12 Avenue du Château de la Malmaison, 92500, Rueil-Malmaison

Located about 10 kilometres west of Paris, this château was the home of Empress Josephine, the first wife of Napoléon Bonaparte. The building is now a museum housing a large collection of Napoleonic memorabilia.

Château de Saint-Germain-en-Laye

1 Place Charles de Gaulle, 78100, Saint-Germain-en-Laye

This château and its adjoining gardens is located about 15 kilometres west of Paris. It was used as a royal residence by French kings from the 11th to the 18th centuries. Today, it houses the National Archaeological Museum.

Château de Vincennes

Avenue de Paris, 94300, Vincennes

This castle, located in the eastern suburbs of Paris, was home to the kings of France between the 14th and 16th centuries. Be sure to visit the Sainte-Chapelle de Vincennes, modelled after the church of the same name in Paris.

Conciergerie

2 Blvd du Palais, 75001, 1st Arr.

Originally part of the Palais de la Cité, the seat of the French monarchy from the 10th to the 14th centuries. From the 14th century onwards it was used as a prison, notably during the French Revolution, when it was used to hold those awaiting trial by the Revolutionary Tribunal. Today, it is a museum offering visitors a glimpse into the past.

Louvre

75001, 1st Arr.

This former royal palace, which was home to the French royal family for centuries, is now one of the largest museums in the world. The original palace was built in the 12th century and its ruins can be seen in the basement of the Louvre. The current palace was built in the 17th century, and today houses a vast collection of art and antiquities from around the world.

Palace of Versailles

Place d'Armes, 78000, Versailles

One of the most popular tourist attractions in France, and with good reason. This opulent baroque palace was the main residence of the French royal family during the 17th and 18th centuries.

Palais-Royal

8 Rue de Montpensier, 75001, 1st Arr.

Built in the 17th century, this palace was home to the Duke of Orléans and then various members of the royal and imperial families as France cycled through governments post-Revolution. It now is a museum with a beautiful public garden.

Luxembourg Palace

15 Rue de Vaugirard, 75006, 6th Arr.

A 17th-century palace located in the 6th arrondissement of Paris. It was originally built for Marie de' Medici, the widow of King Henry IV, as a place to retire from the political intrigues of the French court. The palace is now the seat of the French Senate, the upper house of the French Parliament.

Square de Villa Léandre   Rue Chanoinesse   La Campagne à
Montsouris   Paris

Rue des   Rue de   Rue de l'Abreuvoir   Rue des
Thermopyles   Furstemberg   Barres

Rue Crémieux   Avenue de   Place   Cour du   Rue Sainte-
                Camoëns   Dauphine   Commerce   Marthe
                                          Saint-André

CHARMING STREETS

PARIS BY INTEREST

With centuries of *rich culture* is it no surprise that
Paris is full of enchanting streets and hidden gems.
From bucolic *neighbourhoods* to hidden passageways,
and medieval houses to art deco homes, there is both
breadth and width when it comes to the types of
beautiful streets that give Paris its *unique charm.*

Avenue de Camoëns
75116, 16th Arr.

Known for its view of the Eiffel Tower, this short but charming street is a great place to visit if you want to see the iconic landmark from a different perspective

La Campagne à Paris
75020, 20th Arr.

Situated on a small hilltop, this quiet neighbourhood is known for its charming, cottage-style houses, its narrow cobbled streets and its bucolic atmosphere. While in the neighbourhood be sure to stop by Amie Baguette and La Toute Petite Librairie (the Tiny Bookstore).

Cour du Commerce Saint-André
75006, 6th Arr.

This 12th-century street is steeped in history. As well as being a popular meeting spot for revolutionaries, it is also home to Paris's oldest café, Le Procope, a popular gathering place for writers, artists and philosophers.

Place Dauphine
75001, 1st Arr.

Pick up a pastry from Atelier du Geste à l'Émotion and sit and enjoy the ambience of this square, with its classical French façades.

Rue de l'Abreuvoir
75018, 18th Arr.

Dating back to the 14th century, this is one of the oldest streets in Montmartre. It was the centre of the bohemian art scene with artists such as Picasso, Matisse and Suzanne Valadon living nearby. Home to iconic La Maison Rose, this charming street offers a stunning view of Sacré-Coeur.

Rue des Barres
75004, 4th Arr.

See two of the oldest medieval houses in Paris located a few hundred metres from each other in the Marais. If you are needing a rest, pop into Aux Merveilleux de Fred or Le Peloton Café.

Rue Chanoinesse

75004, 4th Arr.

This street is home to Au Vieux Paris d'Arcole, a charming café in a 16th-century townhouse with wisteria draping its walls in the spring.

Rue Crémieux

75012, 12th Arr.

This residential street is a rainbow of houses that are so cheerfully painted it will make you smile. Have lunch at one of the restaurants at either end of the street, Le Crémieux at one end or Yucos at the other.

Rue de Furstemberg

75006, 6th Arr.

A charming square surrounded by delightful shops. Enjoy the Parisian bouquets at Oz Garden and shop for artisanal salts and spices at Compagnie Française des Poivres et des Épices.

Rue Sainte-Marthe

75010, 10th Arr.

This colourful street is dotted with great restaurants and shops. Some favourites are Crêperie Armorix and Sandra's Kitchen.

Rue des Thermopyles

75014, 14th Arr.

This cobblestoned residential street feels like a world away from Paris. With an abundance of greenery, the street feels like an urban garden and is popular with locals and tourists alike.

Square de Montsouris

75014, 14th Arr.

Built between the 1920s and 30s, this street is known for its art deco architecture and charming atmosphere. Its village vibe and quiet atmosphere makes it a welcome respite from the city centre.

Villa Léandre

75018, 18th Arr.

This cobblestoned cul-de-sac was built in the art deco style of the 1920s. If you are in the area, be sure to visit Boris Lumé Boulangerie for some delicious baked treats.

Arc de
Triomphe

Galeries Lafayette

Jardin Bergeyre

L'Herbarium

Pompidou Centre

Le Jardin
du Raphael

Le Perchoir
Marais

Tour
Saint-
Jacques

Les Ombres

Montparnasse
Tower

Square
Jean
XXIII

BEST VIEWS

Part of the magic of Paris is that no matter where you go, you're bound to find *stunning* views that will take your breath away. But it's not just the views that make Paris *magical*. It's the atmosphere, the people and the energy of the city. There's something about Paris that makes you feel like you're in a *fairy-tale* or an *Impressionist* painting. Better still, some of the best places to view the *sights* of Paris are off the beaten path – from up high to *quiet* parks.

Arc de Triomphe

Place Charles de Gaulle, 75008, 8th Arr.

Climbing to the top of this triumphal arch offers views of the Champs-Élysées and other landmarks in the city centre.

Jardin Bergeyre

Rue Georges Lardennois, 75019, 19th Arr.

The reward of climbing a big flight of stairs is a sweeping view of Paris and a wonderful vantage point from which to see the Sacré-Coeur.

Montparnasse Tower

33 Avenue du Maine, 75015, 15th Arr.

This skyscraper offers the highest views of Paris from its 59th-floor observation deck. The views are especially impressive at night when the city is lit up.

Square Jean XXIII

4 Place du Parvis Notre-Dame, 75004, 4th Arr.

Head to the garden behind Notre-Dame for an equally stunning, and less crowded view of the iconic church.

Tour Saint-Jacques

Square de la Tour Saint-Jacques, 75004, 4th Arr.

This tower is all that remains of the former church that was destroyed during the French Revolution. A climb to the top of this gothic tower offers panoramic views of Paris.

ROOFTOPS WITH A VIEW

Check seasonal hours.

Galeries Lafayette

40 Blvd Haussmann, 75009, 9th Arr.

Enjoy the eighth-floor terrace with panoramic views at this famous department store. To enjoy the ambience a bit longer, have a nice lunch at the vegetarian restaurant here, Créatures.

L'Herbarium

243 Rue Saint-Martin, 75003, 3rd Arr.

Sitting atop the Hôtel National des Arts et Métiers is a cocktail bar offering up great views of the city.

Le Jardin du Raphael

17 Avenue Kléber, 75116, 16th Arr.

Open from May to September, this rooftop at Hôtel Raphael offers stunning views of the Eiffel Tower on one side and the Arc de Triomphe on the other.

Les Ombres

27 Quai Jacques Chirac, 75007, 7th Arr.

An elegant rooftop bar and restaurant situated on top of the Quai Branly–Jacques Chirac museum, and a wonderful place to enjoy a fancy lunch or dinner.

Pompidou Centre

Place Georges Pompidou, 75004, 4th Arr.

This modern art museum has a rooftop restaurant, Le Georges, with panoramic views of Paris.

Le Perchoir Marais

33 Rue de la Verrerie, 75004, 4th Arr.

Sitting atop the BHV Marais department store is this rooftop cocktail bar. With skyline views and signature cocktails it is a lovely place to spend a few hours.

Science and
Industry Museum

Jardin
d'Acclimatation

Shops for
Children

Jardin
d'Acclimatation

Champ de
Mars

Carousels

Miniature
France

Luxembourg
Gardens

Jardin des
Plantes

CHILDREN'S PARIS

Paris is an exciting place to explore with kids of all ages. There are so many *wonderful museums*, playgrounds, parks and green spaces, leaving you spoilt for choice when it comes to deciding what to do. My biggest piece of advice when *travelling* with kids, especially in a big city, is not to overdo it. Pick one or two activities the kids will enjoy and *intersperse* that with your own preferences. And, if all else fails, I find a visit to a playground or a park is always a good plan. I've spent an entire day at *Parisian playgrounds* with my daughter while on holiday and have met some lovely locals, who often have great suggestions of places to eat and explore.

Carousels
Multiple locations

Paris is full of charming carousels and no two are alike. For a merry-go-round with a stunning view, visit the Jardin du Trocadéro or Place Saint-Pierre in Montmartre. For a small carousel, go to Square Boucicaut.

Champ de Mars
75007, 7th Arr.

With unimpeded views of the nearby Eiffel Tower, this park is a popular place for locals and tourists alike. There is a small playground that is ideal for younger children, a marionette theatre and ample green space to set up your perfect picnic spread.

Luxembourg Gardens
75006 Paris, 6th Arr.

These beautiful gardens have ample things for families to explore and enjoy. There is a puppet theatre, botanical garden, amazing kids' playground and model sailboats to hire that children can 'sail' around the fountain.

Jardin des Plantes
75005, 5th Arr.

Explore one of the oldest botanical gardens in the world, with over 10,000 different plant species. Visit one of the many museums dotted around the garden. The Evolution Gallery is home to a vast collection of animal specimens, while the Gallery of Paleontology houses a collection of fossils of dinosaurs and other prehistoric animals. The garden's own zoo is home to over 1,000 animals from around the world, including lions, tigers, elephants and giraffes.

Jardin d'Acclimatation

Bois de Boulogne, 16th Arr.

The first amusement park in France
is still a firm favourite with children
and families today. With delightful
rides, a petting zoo and boating
lake, it is a great place to enjoy a
fun day out.

Miniature France

Blvd André Malraux, 78990, Élancourt

About 40 kilometres outside Paris is this charming theme park with
miniature replicas of France's famous buildings and landmarks. It is
fun to explore and see the amazing detail and craftsmanship on each
of the mini monuments.

Science and Industry Museum

30 Avenue Corentin Cariou, 75019, 19th Arr.

One of the biggest science museums in Europe, the Cité des Sciences et de
l'Industrie (CSI) offers up lots of interactive and hands-on exhibits, perfect
for getting children interested and engaged.

Shops for Children

Multiple locations

Paris has some incredible shops for kids' clothing. Be sure to check out
Bonton, Smallable, Centre Commercial Kids for clothing and Si Tu Veux,
Le Petit Local, Moulin Roty and Lulu & Cie for toys.

Musée Jacquemart André

Fondation Louis Vuitton

Gustave Moreau
Museum

Musée Marmottan Monet

Musée de
l'Orangerie

Museum of
Decorative Arts

Picasso
Museum

Modern Art Museum/
Palais de Tokyo

Louvre

Pompidou Centre

Rodin Museum

Musée d'Orsay

Cluny Museum

Curie Museum

MUSEUMS

Paris has more museums than any other city in the world.
With over 130 museums in the city covering a wide range
of subjects, from art and history to *science* and *technology,*
they make Paris a must-visit destination for any art lover
or *cultural* enthusiast. During the *French Revolution*
the vast collection of art and artefacts owned by the royal
family were entrusted to the nation as *royal properties*
were nationalized. These residences became museums and
are still enjoyed by tourists today. There is no way you can
explore all the museums in one visit! It is best to do your
research and visit those that *interest you* especially. Also, it
is okay to not do the Louvre. If you want to, great, but there
is no rule saying that you must.

Cluny Museum

28 Rue du Sommerard, 75005, 5th Arr.

Home to a notable collection of art from the Middle Ages, including the iconic series of six 15th-century tapestries known as *The Lady and the Unicorn*.

Curie Museum

1 Rue Pierre et Marie Curie, 75005, 5th Arr.

Former laboratory turned museum celebrating Marie Curie, the pioneering scientist and Nobel prize winner, and the history of radioactivity.

Fondation Louis Vuitton

8 Avenue du Mahatma Gandhi, 75116, 16th Arr.

This striking building by Frank Gehry houses a wonderful collection of contemporary art.

Gustave Moreau Museum

14 Rue Catherine de la Rochefoucauld, 75009, 9th Arr.

This art museum in Moreau's former home houses one of the largest collections of works by Symbolist painter Gustave Moreau.

Louvre

75001, 1st Arr.

The largest museum in the world, this vast museum is a true labyrinth, with treasures around every corner.

Modern Art Museum / Palais de Tokyo

11/13 Avenue du Président Wilson, 75116, 16th Arr.

These two neighbouring museums are dedicated to modern art. Palais de Tokyo hosts temporary exhibitions and events, while the Modern Art Museum has a permanent collection of contemporary art.

Musée de l'Orangerie

Jardin des Tuileries, 75001, 1st Arr.

This museum houses panoramic *Waterlilies* murals by Claude Monet, which were specially commissioned for this space. The museum's collection should be on everyone's Paris itinerary.

Musée d'Orsay
Esplanade Valéry Giscard d'Estaing, 75007, 7th Arr.
This museum is home to some of the most famous works from Impressionist and Post-Impressionist artists. It is a must-see for fans of this era.

Musée Jacquemart-André
158 Blvd Haussmann, 75008, 8th Arr.
Housed in the former 19th-century mansion of Édouard André and Nélie Jacquemart, the rooms are adorned with their period furniture and outstanding collection of Italian Renaissance art.

Musée Marmottan Monet
2 Rue Louis Boilly, 75016, 16th Arr.
Dedicated to the work of Claude Monet, it houses the largest collection of his work, as well art from his personal collection.

Museum of Decorative Arts
107 Rue de Rivoli, 75001, 1st Arr.
The expansive collection, covering from the Middle Ages to the present day, includes furniture, textiles, ceramics, glassware, jewellery, fashion and costume design from around the world. Its beautiful setting makes it a truly unique experience.

Picasso Museum
5 Rue de Thorigny, 75003, 3rd Arr.
With over 5,000 pieces arranged chronologically, this museum covers all of Picasso's artistic periods and houses some of most famous works.

Rodin Museum
77 Rue de Varenne, 75007, 7th Arr.
Former home turned museum dedicated to the works of the sculptor Auguste Rodin. Some of Rodin's most famous works are on display here.

Pompidou Centre
Place Georges Pompidou, 75004, 4th Arr.
Home to the largest collection of modern art in Europe, where the building is as much part of the art as the collection. The high-tech architectural building was the first 'inside-out' building created on a large scale.

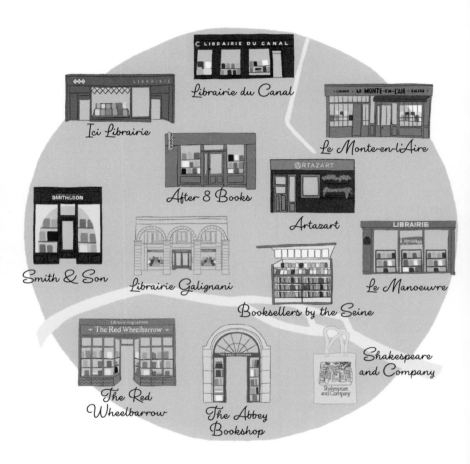

Librairie du Canal

Ici Librairie

Le Monte-en-l'Aire

After 8 Books

Artazart

Smith & Son

Librairie Galignani

Le Manoeuvre

Booksellers by the Seine

The Red Wheelbarrow

The Abbey Bookshop

Shakespeare and Company

BOOKSTORES

The bookstores of Paris are some of the most beautiful, *inspiring writers* from around the world for centuries. From the iconic Shakespeare and Company to the hidden gems of the *Latin Quarter*, there is something special about browsing the shelves of a Parisian bookstore. Whether you are a seasoned *bibliophile* or a casual reader, visiting a *librairie* in Paris is a must-do for any visitor. It is a chance to experience the city's rich *literary history*, to discover new titles, and simply lose yourself in the *world of books* in a city that is full of inspiration. And if you don't read French, don't worry – there are several shops that *specialize* in English-language books, and most carry a small selection of foreign-edition books.

The Abbey Bookshop

29 Rue de la Parcheminerie, 75005, 5th Arr.

A treasure trove of English-language books in the heart of Paris selling new, used and rare tomes.

After 8 Books

7 Rue Jarry, 75010, 10th Arr.

Great curation of interesting and unique titles. It is the perfect place to find the atypical.

Artazart

83 Quai de Valmy, 75010, 10th Arr.

This delightful bookstore boasts a large collection of graphic design books, children's books and books on photography as well as a wonderful assortment of prints from different artists.

Booksellers by the Seine

Right bank: Pont Marie to the Louvre

Left bank: Quai de la Tournelle to Quai Voltaire

There is a certain excitement to browsing the second-hand bookstalls or bouquinistes nestled along the banks of the Seine, with their seemingly endless rows of old books, maps and prints. There are hidden treasures to be found in each one.

Ici Librairie

25 Blvd Poissonnière, 75002, 2nd Arr.

A neighbourhood favourite boasting a wide selection of books, it is the perfect to spend an afternoon browsing the shelves.

Librairie du Canal

3 Rue Eugène Varlin, 75010, 20th Arr.

Charming bookshop along the Canal Saint-Martin filled with treasures for book lovers of all ages.

Librairie Galignani
224 Rue de Rivoli, 75001, 1st Arr.
Located in a historic setting just across from the Tuileries Garden, this beautiful bookstore has a wide selection of books in English and French.

La Manoeuvre
58 Rue de la Roquette, 75011, 11th Arr.
A delightful children's bookshop with a great selection of new and rare children's books. They also have a great kids' story time for young ones.

Le Monte-en-l'Air
2 Rue de la Mare, 75020, 20th Arr.
An incredible repository of unique books with an emphasis on philosophy, design, photography and photo art books from all over the world.

Shakespeare and Company
37 Rue de la Bûcherie, 75005, 5th Arr.
Located in the heart of the Latin Quarter, this bookshop is a must-visit for any book lover in Paris. It is known for its literary associations, having been a gathering place for writers and artists such as Hemingway and F. Scott Fitzgerald.

Smith & Son
248 Rue de Rivoli, 75001, 1st Arr.
English bookshop with a tea shop serving up scones alongside classic novels and the latest releases.

The Red Wheelbarrow
9 and 11 Rue de Médicis, 75006, 6th Arr.
More relaxed and less crowded than other English bookshops in Paris, but with a wonderful selection of carefully curated books.

PARIS

BY SEASON

PART FOUR

PARIS IN SPRING + PARIS IN SUMMER + ROMANTIC PARIS +

PARIS IN AUTUMN + PARIS IN WINTER + FESTIVE TREATS +

TIPS FOR EXPLORING PARIS

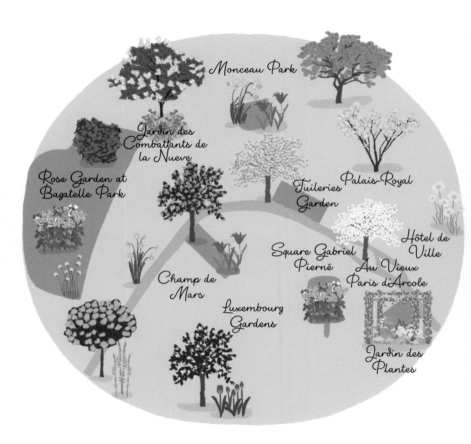

Monceau Park

Jardin des
Combattants de
la Nueve

Rose Garden at
Bagatelle Park

Palais-Royal

Tuileries
Garden

Hôtel de
Ville

Square Gabriel
Pierné

Au Vieux
Paris d'Arcole

Champ de
Mars

Luxembourg
Gardens

Jardin des
Plantes

PARIS IN SPRING

PARIS BY SEASON

In spring, Paris is *transformed* by the cherry blossoms, magnolias and other spring flowers filling the parks, gardens and streets. The *colourful blooms* are a welcome respite from the cold winter weather and a *reminder* of the warmer days ahead. From February to March, keep an eye out for *daffodils*; in April and May, look for *cherry blossom* and magnolias; in May, it's tulip time; and from June, *roses* will be in bloom.

Jardin des Plantes
57 Rue Cuvier, 75005, 5th Arr.
Botanical garden with blossoms
throughout the spring.

Champ de Mars
75007, 7th Arr.
Cherry blossom.

Hôtel de Ville
Place de l'Hôtel-de-Ville, 75004, 4th Arr.
Cherry blossom.

Jardin des Combattants de la Nueve
1341 Quai de l'Hôtel de Ville, 75004, 4th Arr.
Cherry blossom, magnolias, roses.

Luxembourg Gardens
75006 Paris, 6th Arr.
Cherry blossom, roses, planted flowerbeds.

Monceau Park
35 Blvd de Courcelles, 75008, 8th Arr.
Daffodils, cherry blossom, roses.

Palais-Royal
2 Gal de Montpensier, 75001, 1st Arr.
Magnolias.

Square Gabriel Pierné
5 Rue de Seine, 75006, 6th Arr.
Cherry blossom.

Tuileries Garden
Place de la Concorde, 75001, 1st Arr.
Cherry blossom.

Au Vieux Paris d'Arcole
24 Rue Chanoinesse, 75004, 4th Arr.
This restaurant near Notre-Dame is covered with
wisteria – visit in spring and early summer to see it.

Rose Garden at Bagatelle Park
42 Route de Sèvres à Neuilly, 75016, 16th Arr.
This is the largest rose garden in Paris, open from
April to October.

Bagatelle Park

Monceau Park

Tuileries Garden

Belleville Park

Buttes-Chaumont Park

Île aux Cygnes

Trocadéro Gardens

Square du Vert-Galant

Place des Vosges

Bois de Vincennes

Luxembourg Gardens

Jardin des Plantes

Georges Brassens Park

Montsouris Park

PARIS IN SUMMER

PARIS BY SEASON

From the formal Luxembourg Gardens to the *wilder expanses* of the Bois de Vincennes, there is a park here for everyone to *enjoy*, whether you want a leisurely stroll, a place to take your *children* to play or somewhere to gather with friends and family for a *picnic or game*. Paris's parks and gardens are the perfect *getaway* from crowded museums and other attractions.

Bagatelle Park

42 Route de Sèvres à Neuilly, 75016, 16th Arr.
Located within the Bois de Boulogne, this
landscaped park boasts peacocks and a waterfall.

Belleville Park

47 Rue des Couronnes, 75020, 20th Arr.
This hilltop park offers sweeping views of Paris.

Bois de Vincennes

75012, 12th Arr.
Filled with things to enjoy, with a zoo, botanical gardens, walking and
biking trails and a lake.

Buttes-Chaumont Park

75019, 19th Arr.
Featuring a lake, a waterfall, a grotto and a small temple.

Georges Brassens Park

2 Place Jacques Marette, 75015, 15th Arr.
Boasting a pond, sculptures and a small carousel for children.

Île aux Cygnes

75007, 7th Arr.
You can find a mini Statue of Liberty (one of five in Paris) in this park
within the Champ de Mars.

Jardin des Plantes

57 Rue Cuvier, 75005, 5th Arr.
Wonderful garden with a zoo, maze and botanical gardens.

Luxembourg Gardens

75006, 6th Arr.

Formal gardens with a playground and another miniature
Statue of Liberty.

Monceau Park

35 Blvd de Courcelles, 75008, 8th Arr.

Enjoy the colonnade and pyramid follies this park offers.

Montsouris Park

2 Rue Gazan, 75014, 14th Arr.

An English landscape-style garden, with a lake and wide sloping lawns.

Place des Vosges

75004, 4th Arr.

The oldest planned square in Paris, it remains much unchanged since
it was built in 1612.

Square du Vert-Galant

15 Place du Pont Neuf, 75001, 1st Arr.

Sitting in the middle of the Seine, this park offers lovely views of Paris.

Trocadéro Gardens

Place du Trocadéro et du 11 Novembre, 75016, 16th Arr.

Lovely fountains and stunning views of the Eiffel Tower.

Tuileries Garden

Place de la Concorde, 75001, 1st Arr.

Iconic tree-lined garden filled with
statues – and chairs for relaxing and
enjoying the atmosphere.

Bois de
Boulogne

Photobooth

Petite
Museum

Rooftop
Bar

Neighbourhood
Stroll

Eiffel
Tower

Picnic in
a Park

ROMANTIC PARIS

Idealized by the *Impressionists*, written about by dreamers and revitalized by the Revolutionaries, Paris has had a *romantic air* about it for centuries. The city's picturesque backdrops include stunning centuries-old architecture from gothic churches to *Renaissance* palaces, the baroque and Rococo embellishments of the eighteenth century and the *Haussmannian* buildings that fill the streets today. Pair that with exquisite food and drink, *Belle Époque* cafés and brasseries, and the result is an atmosphere that can't be found anywhere else in the world. To *embrace the charm* of the city, avoid the over-touristed spots, and instead find your own romantic Paris.

Take a Romantic Neighbourhood Stroll

Stroll the streets of Montmartre; walk the Rue des Barres in the Marais; or stroll along the Seine, stopping for a drink along the way.

Enjoy a Petite Museum

Paris has over 100 museums, and the small ones are delightful to explore. Consider the Albert-Kahn Museum and Garden, the Museum of Romantic Life, the wonderful sculpture garden at the Rodin Museum or the giant Monet waterlilies at the Musée de l'Orangerie.

Savour a Picnic in a Park

A picnic in a beautiful park is a wonderful way to experience the romance of Paris. Stop by a local fromagerie or boulangerie to pick up an easy meal to enjoy. Some wonderful spots for a picnic are Canal Saint-Martin, Luxembourg Palace and Gardens or the Champ de Mars.

Have a Drink at a Rooftop Bar

Admire the city from these venues with a view.

La Suite Girafe, 1 Place du Trocadéro et du 11 Novembre, 75016, 16th Arr.
With stunning views of the Eiffel Tower, this is the perfect place to enjoy a quiet evening with your favourite someone.

Rooftop Bar Villa M, 28 Blvd Pasteur, 75015, 15th Arr.
Sweeping views and a great place to enjoy a drink and watch the sun set.

Visit a Photobooth

There are a handful of vintage-style photobooths (fotoautomats) dotted around the city. They are the perfect place to get a romantic souvenir. You can find them here:

Palais de Tokyo, 16th Arr.

Café Caché, Le Centquatre, 19th Arr.

Kids' concept store Bonton, 14th Arr.

Near the fruit and veg shops, 53 Rue des Trois Frères, Montmartre, 18th Arr.

Outside Le Pavillon Puebla restaurant, Buttes-Chaumont Park, 19th Arr.

Paris Philharmonic Concert Halls, 221 Avenue Jean Jaurès, 19th Arr.

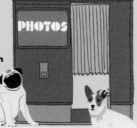

Explore the Bois de Boulogne

This expansive park in the 16th arrondissement is a great place to walk. With gardens, cafés and restaurants dotted throughout, you can enjoy a leisurely stroll and escape the bustle of the city.

Watch the Eiffel Tower at Night

This one is a cliché, but it is also a must-do! Bonus points if you are eating a crêpe while it sparkles on the hour.

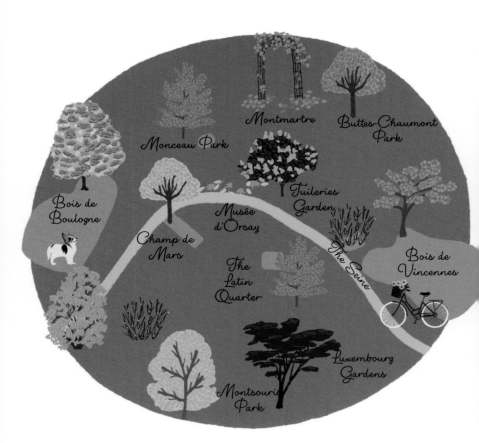

Monceau Park

Montmartre

Buttes-Chaumont
Park

Bois de
Boulogne

Tuileries
Garden

Musée
d'Orsay

Champ de
Mars

The Seine

Bois de
Vincennes

The
Latin
Quarter

Luxembourg
Gardens

Montsouris
Park

PARIS IN AUTUMN

Autumn is a wonderful time to visit Paris. The weather is cooler but not too cold, and the *colourful foliage* in the parks and tree-lined streets is spectacular. As the leaves on the trees turn to *vibrant* shades of yellow, orange and red, the city's parks are transformed into a *kaleidoscope* of colour. This is the *perfect season* to take a walk, have a picnic or simply enjoy the transformed views.

Bois de Boulogne
75016, 16th Arr.
This large park has woodland trails that turn vibrant hues in the autumn.

Bois de Vincennes
Route de la Pyramide, 75012, 12th Arr.
This forest in the east of Paris is a great place to go for a long walk or bike ride in crisp weather.

Buttes-Chaumont Park
75019, 19th Arr.
With ample tree-lined paths and walkways, this park becomes stunningly gorgeous in the autumn.

Musée d'Orsay
Esplanade Valéry Giscard d'Estaing, 75007, 7th Arr.
This museum is a wonderful vantage point to view beautiful autumn foliage across the Seine.

Champ de Mars
75007, 7th Arr.
This large grassy field located at the foot of the Eiffel Tower is a great place to enjoy the autumn leaves in an iconic setting.

The Latin Quarter
5th Arr.
This historic neighbourhood has an abundance of narrow streets and cafés, which are lined with foliage.

Luxembourg Gardens
75006, 6th Arr.
Home to a variety of trees including maples, oaks and chestnuts, which all turn stunning shades of red, orange and yellow in the autumn.

Monceau Park

35 Blvd de Courcelles, 75008, 8th Arr.

This elegant park is a great place to see autumn colours.

Montmartre

9th Arr.

This idyllic neighbourhood is so charming in the autumn, with some of the best foliage on Rue Saint-Vincent, Rue des Thermopyles, Rue de l'Abreuvoir and at Montmartre Vineyard.

Montsouris Park

2 Rue Gazan, 75014, 14th Arr.

An English landscape-style garden by Jean-Charles Adolphe Alphand, with a lake and wide sloping lawns.

The Seine

The river Seine that runs through Paris is lined with trees – stroll along and admire the change of seasons.

Tuileries Garden

Place de la Concorde, 75001, 1st Arr.

This beautiful tree-lined garden turns intense yellow in the autumn.

Ice
Skating

Seasonal
Concerts

Christmas
Markets

Christmas
Lights

PARIS IN WINTER

PARIS BY SEASON

Winter here is a *magical time*. The city is decorated for the holidays and there are ample activities to enjoy, from *ice skating* and Christmas markets to visiting museums and enjoying the *seasonal* shop window displays. Although the weather is chilly, there is no denying the *charm and delight* of winter in Paris. It is a *perfect* time to wrap up, slow down and *savour* the city's beauty.

Christmas Markets

Christmas Markets have been part of Parisian history for centuries. They are fun to browse for gifts and there is always delicious food and drinks to keep you warm. Find them here:

Eiffel Tower

Hôtel de Ville

Montmartre

Notre-Dame

Tuileries Garden

Ice Skating

Set in iconic places, these temporary ice rinks are a fun way to enjoy a winter afternoon; and afterwards you will deserve a rest in a café with a hot chocolate! Locations sometimes vary from year to year, but they can generally be found here:

Champs-Élysées

Eiffel Tower

Grand Palais des Glaces

Tuileries Garden

Christmas Lights

Head to the big department stores for stunning installations or wander the narrower streets to delight in the décor on a smaller scale. The Champs-Élysées are always adorned with spectacular lights, and don't miss Place Vendôme, Avenue Montaigne, Galeries Lafayette stores, the Bercy neighbourhood, Le Village Royal shopping area or the Jardin des Plantes light trail.

Seasonal Concerts

Enjoy a festive concert in one of Paris's iconic churches (*églises*), from Sainte-Chapelle to Église Saint-Germain-des-Prés, Église de la Madeleine, Saint-Sulpice, Saint-Eustache and even Handel's *Messiah* at the American Cathedral. There are countless places to enjoy Christmas choral music.

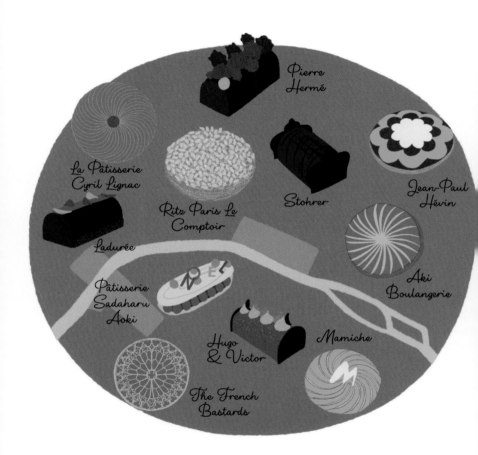

Pierre Hermé

La Pâtisserie Cyril Lignac

Ritz Paris Le Comptoir

Stohrer

Jean-Paul Hévin

Ladurée

Pâtisserie Sadaharu Aoki

Aki Boulangerie

Hugo & Victor

Mamiche

The French Bastards

FESTIVE TREATS

From early December until *Twelfth Night* you can find delicious festive treats at the boulangeries and pâtisseries of Paris. Two very seasonal desserts are *Bûche de Noël* and *Galette des Rois*. The former derives from the original *yule log* that was traditionally burned at the winter solstice as a celebration of the days lengthening again. Galette des Rois is enjoyed to celebrate *Epiphany* (6 January) and to bring *good luck* into the following year. A small figurine, called a *fève*, is hidden inside the cake and whoever finds it is said to be king or queen for the day. Both the Bûche de Noël and the Galette des Rois are *delicious* and rich in history and tradition – not to be missed if you are in Paris during the festive season.

Aki Boulangerie
16 Rue Sainte-Anne, 75001, 1st Arr.
Galette des Rois.

The French Bastards
Multiple locations
Galette des Rois.

Hugo & Victor
40 Blvd Raspail, 75007, 7th Arr.
Bûche de Noël.

Jean-Paul Hévin
Multiple locations
Galette des Rois.

Ladurée
Multiple locations
Bûche de Noël.

Mamiche
45 Rue Condorcet, 75009, 9th Arr.
Galette des Rois.

La Pâtisserie Cyril Lignac
Multiple locations
Galette des Rois.

Pâtisserie Sadaharu Aoki
Multiple locations
Bûche de Noël.

Pierre Hermé
Multiple locations
Bûche de Noël and Galette des Rois.

Ritz Paris Le Comptoir
38 Rue Cambon, 75001, 1st Arr.
Galette des Rois.

Stohrer
Multiple locations
Bûche de Noël.

TIPS FOR EXPLORING PARIS

I hope you find inspiration in these illustrations. Paris has been a thriving city for millennia and there will always be something more to explore. There is no 'right' way to explore Paris; the perfect trip is the trip that involves doing things that you value when travelling.

Here are things to think about to ensure you get the best from your time in Paris, whether you are a first-time visitor or a well-seasoned traveller.

1. A little bit of French goes a long way. I'd highly recommend learning how to say a few things beyond *Bonjour* and *Merci*.

2. Say *Bonjour* when you enter a shop, café or restaurant. It is considered quite rude not to. It is also customary to say *Au revoir* and *Merci* when leaving smaller shops, cafés or restaurants.

3. What is important to you when you take a holiday? Are you looking to relax? Explore neighbourhoods like a local? Whatever the answer to this question is, make sure you prioritize that for your trip.

4. Wear practical shoes. Paris is very walkable, and you can easily find yourself walking over 20,000 steps a day. Parisians are practical people, so wear practical shoes.

5. Take time to enjoy the atmosphere. Make sure you put your phone and camera down and just enjoy the views and sites. Paris has an amazing café culture, so take advantage of sitting, people watching and enjoying a drink or a meal.

6. Reserve restaurants in advance when you can. Lots of places do take walk-ins and this would be a good opportunity to use any French you know to ask politely if they have a table available.

7. Don't try to do everything. Pick a few things and do them well; you won't be disappointed.

Published in 2024 by OH
An imprint of Welbeck Publishing Group.
Offices in: London — 20 Mortimer Street, London W1T 3JW &
Sydney — Level 17, 207 Kent St, Sydney NSW 2000 Australia
www.welbeckpublishing.com

Design © 2024 Welbeck Publishing Group
Text © 2024 Cierra Block
Illustrations © 2024 Cierra Block

A CIP catalogue record for this book is available from the British Library.

ISBN 978 1 80453 105 1

Publisher: Lisa Dyer
Copyeditor: Clare Double
Designer: Lucy Palmer
Illustrator: Cierra Block
Production controller: Arlene Lestrade

Printed and bound by RR Donnelley in China

MIX
Paper | Supporting
responsible forestry
FSC® C144853

10 9 8 7 6 5 4 3 2 1

Note: Readers will notice that there is a combination of French and Anglicized place names.
We have decided to follow rules of convention and retain the French spellings when English
speakers are familiar with the French word and likely to use the original language rather
than the English translation.

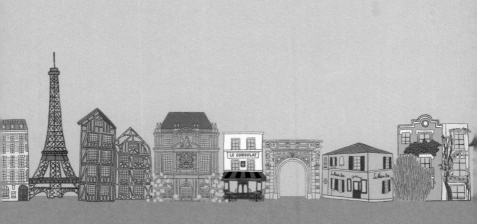